HOW TO GET KIDS OFFLINE, OUTDOORS,
AND CONNECTING WITH NATURE

HOW TO GET KIDS
OFFLINE,
OUTDOORS,
AND CONNECTING
WITH NATURE

200+ CREATIVE ACTIVITIES TO ENCOURAGE SELF-ESTEEM, MINDFULNESS, AND WELLBEING

BONNIE THOMAS

Jessica Kingsley *Publishers*
London and Philadelphia

Health and Safety Disclaimer

Before trying out any of the activities described in this book, readers should check they understand and can comply fully with the health and safety regulations and risk assessment requirements that govern outdoor activities with children. Neither the author nor the publisher take any responsibility for any consequences of any action taken as a result of the information contained in this book.

First published in 2014
by Jessica Kingsley Publishers
73 Collier Street
London N1 9BE, UK
and
400 Market Street, Suite 400
Philadelphia, PA 19106, USA

www.jkp.com

Library of Congress Cataloging in Publication Data
Thomas, Bonnie, 1971-
    How to get kids offline, outdoors, and connecting with nature : 200+ Creative activities to encourage
self-esteem, mindfulness, and wellbeing/ Bonnie Thomas
        pages cm.
  ISBN 978-1-84905-968-8 (alk. paper)
  1. Outdoor recreation for children. I. Title.
  GV191.63.T56 2013
  796.083--dc23
                                        2013032891

British Library Cataloguing in Publication Data
A CIP catalogue record for this book is available from the British Library

ISBN 978 1 84905 968 8
eISBN 978 0 85700 853 4

Printed and bound in Great Britain

ACKNOWLEDGMENTS

I have such gratitude for each and every person who helped me complete *How to Get Kids Offline, Outdoors, and Connecting with Nature*. Many people contributed written excerpts, photographs, artwork, or let me use photos of their children—all of which made this book more rich and dynamic than I had hoped for.

Thank you SO very much to: Bryan and Alyssa Wolf at Squeaky Wheel Adventures, Lori Krupke at Kids' Corner, Karla Helbert LPC, Kirsten Hardy, Pamela Tachibana at ArtSwarm, Megan Emery, Heather Mladek Photography, Lauren Verow, Michelle Guertin, Aimee Vlachos, Kristen Davis, Eileen Pastorelli, Lucy King, Jennifer O'Neil, Karin Gibson, Julia Birtolo, Alexandra Sagov, Li Luo, Hilary Denvir, Susan Landgrebe, Rachel and John Burke, Ami Esquivel, Ryan Sayer, Sarah Nunan and Laurie Foes of Laurie Made at Etsy.

CONTENTS

Introduction: Why is nature so important?. 11

PART I NATURE IS THERAPEUTIC 15

Chapter 1. Incorporating Nature in Your Therapeutic Practice. 17

Storytelling Stones; Emotion/Emoticon Stones; Talking Sticks; Wishing Wands; Nature-Themed Family Portraits; Worry and Wish Dolls; Wish Books

Chapter 2. Relaxation and Mindfulness 43

Nature-Based Collections; Guided Imagery; Nature Mobiles; Dream Catchers; Nature Collages; Animal Totem Shrines; Portable Zen Garden; Portable Green Gardens; Alphabet Trees; Dandelion Puffs; Labyrinths and Walking Meditations; Stone Stacking; Liquid Sand Sculptures; Painting Stones with Water; Mindfulness in Natural Spaces

Chapter 3. Self-Esteem and Positive Connections 74

Message Stones; Collaged Heart Stones; Square Feet; Earth Looms; Bird Treats; Nesting Shop

Chapter 4. Nature-Based Therapy and Grief Work with Youth by Karla Helbert. 91

Water Painting; Shadow Drawing; Tree Meditation; Journey to the Center of the Earth

Chapter 5. Gardening for Wellbeing. 104

Outdoor Themed Gardens; Rock Gardens; Mini Sculpture Gardens; Community Gardens; Indoor Gardens; Terrariums; Domed Plant Worlds; Windowsill Gardens; Mini.Lawn for Your Feet; Whimsical Container Gardens

PART II NATURE IS FUN 131

Chapter 6. General Outdoor Activities. 133

*Scavenger Hunts; Nature Journals and Sketchbooks; Plein Air
Art; Miniature Outside Worlds; Backyard Play Kitchens; Picnics;
Letterboxing; Geocaching; Camping; National and State Parks;
Public Trails and Historical Places; Farms; Night Time Play and
Observation*

Chapter 7. Blacktop Activities. 161

*Interactive Chalk Landscapes; 3D Chalk Drawings; Chalk Photo
Booth; Rain Silhouettes; Color Bricks; Nature-Based Urban Art;
Hopscotch and Other Blacktop Games*

Chapter 8. Sand and Beach 168

*Sand Sculptures; Edge of the Tide Sculptures and Drawings;
Sand Castles; Pictures in the Sand Using Found Objects; Silly
Shadow Portraits; Shadow Tag; Dragon Tails and Mermaid Hair;
Hangman, Hopscotch, and Tic Tac Toe; Beach Teepee; Beach
Bakery or Bistro; Hum for a Periwinkle; Pop Seaweed; Squirt Clams;
Striped Stone Circles; Beachcombing; Bury Yourself in the Sand;
Sand Angels; Sand Silhouettes*

Chapter 9. Forest and Trees 182

*Climbing Trees; Maple Seed Helicopters; Maple Seed Noses and
Beards; Leaf Crowns; Leaf Chains and Garlands; Tree Art; Willow
Branch Crowns; Apple Faces; Acorn-Cap Finger Puppets; Leaf Pile
Jumping; Pathways in Fallen Leaves; Fairy Wings; Forest Treasures*

Chapter 10. Fields and Grassy Areas 194

*Tumble and Roll; Flour Lawn Pictures; Four-Leaf Clover Hunt;
Pathways in the Fields; Flower Chains; Flower Crowns; Cattail
Plants Swords*

Chapter 11. Puddles and Mud 200

*Puddle Jumping; Puddle Tracing with Chalk; River Making;
Miniature Water World or Marina; Construction Sites and Truck
Baths; Ice Cube Boats; Mud Cakes and Mud Pies; "Fossil" Dig; Mud Bricks*

Chapter 12. Rivers and Streams 206

Bridge Hunt; Boat Building; Pooh Sticks; Dam Building;
Salamander, Snail, and Bug Hunt; Splash and Wade

Chapter 13. Snow 212

Snow Sculptures; Snow People; Snow Insects and Animals; Fantasy
Snow Creatures; Snow Forts and Igloos; Snow Furniture; Pathways
and Patterns in the Snow; Snow Tunnels; Snowball Sculptures;
Snowball Fight; Snow Angels; Snowflakes on Your Tongue;
Snowflakes on a Dark Surface; Frozen Bubbles; Frozen Puddles; Icy
Snow Carving; Ice Lanterns; Mini Castles made with Ice Cubes and Icicles

Chapter 14. Bring Nature Indoors. 234

Clay Insects; Driftwood Cities; Abstract Stones; Stone Magnets;
Indoor Nature-Inspired Garlands; Prisms; Nature Station; Insect
Houses; Miniature Sandboxes; Web Cam Wildlife Watching;
Nature Sounds; Creating with Leaves; Creating with Sticks; Creating
with Flowers; Creating with Seeds and Legumes

REFERENCES 261
ALPHABETICAL LIST OF ACTIVITIES 262

INTRODUCTION
WHY IS NATURE SO IMPORTANT?

I am a mother of a teenager. I am also a counselor who works with families and children. If I can reiterate one point from my experience at either end, it would be that children and teenagers benefit from connecting to nature and unplugging from the chaos of high-stress schedules and excessive screen time. Nature is good for all of us. Sunshine, fresh air, wildlife, plant life, getting our hands in the dirt, walking outdoors, and so on have a positive influence on our wellbeing and mental health.

As a parent I wanted to write this book to assist other parents (and people who care for children) with ideas for engaging our collective youth in the natural world. As a counselor I wanted to write the book to help other social work professionals navigate the "red tape" around incorporating nature-based interventions in treatment goals. Overall it is a "how to" book—how to get kids more connected to nature, and how to help professionals in the mental health field add more nature-based activities in the work they do with clients.

Chapters 1 to 4 are aimed at professionals who work with youth in social work settings—both clinical and general social work. It is written to help these providers incorporate nature-based activity into their practices. Connections to nature are often overlooked in the mental health field and my aim is to help create a shift where more counselors and community workers are helping youth improve their wellbeing through nature-based activity.

Chapters 5 to 14 can also be used by parents and care providers. When I say "parents and care providers" I am referring to the community of people who are raising our children. This includes the parents, extended family, babysitters, daycare teachers, camp counselors, recreation instructors, youth group workers, foster parents, neighbors, school teachers, team coaches, and so on. Anyone who works with children, takes care of children, raises children, or teaches children can get something out of this section of the book. The parent and care provider section will offer many ideas for getting kids connected to nature in fun, creative ways.

As human beings we have lived in and relied on nature for over a million years. It's only in recent history that humans have had television, internet, electronic handheld devices, and technology that allow us access to news, information, friends, and family at any given time. As life has accelerated and screen time has increased, we are collectively leaving our connection to nature behind. Selhub and Logan report, "A recent study in *The Proceedings of the National Academy of Sciences* indicates that overall nature-based recreation has decreased 50 percent in the last four decades" (Selhub and Logan 2012, p.53). Many children are "plugged in" with faces bent down, staring into handheld devices from game devices to the latest technical gadgets. This disconnection from nature is taking its toll. Louv notes "that a young adult living in North America today has a 1-in-4 chance of depression, versus 1-in-10 odds of just two generations ago" (Louv 2008, p.40). Although variable factors could effect this trend, there is no doubt in my mind that reduced time in nature-based play and natural settings is playing a role in the increase in depression, and other mental health illnesses, among our youth.

Overall, people instinctively understand that fresh air, sunshine, healthy foods, and exercise will lead to improved wellbeing. Below are just a few examples of how simple nature-based activities can help. You will find many more ways to bring nature-based pursuits into your work and play with children later in the book.

GO BAREFOOT

Going barefoot is also called "earthing" and "grounding." Clinton Ober, Stephen T. Sinatra, MD and Martin Zucker have written a book called *Earthing: The most important health discovery ever?* in which they explore the benefits of earthing.

> Connecting to the earth—either by being barefooted outside or in contact with a grounded device inside—doesn't cure you of any disease or condition. What it does is to reunite you with the natural electrical signals from the earth that govern all organisms

dwelling upon it. It restores your body's natural internal electrical stability and rhythms, which in turn promote normal functioning of body systems, including the cardiovascular, respiratory, digestive, and immune systems. It remedies an electron deficiency to reduce inflammation—the common cause of disease. It shifts the nervous system from a stress dominated mode to one of calmness and helps you sleep better. By reconnecting, you enable your body to return to its normal electrical state, better able to self-regulate and self-heal. (Ober, Sinatra, and Zucker 2010, p.12)

Encourage your children to get time each day outdoors to walk barefoot or sit on the ground if possible.

GO FOR A WALK

Getting outside for a walk not only gives you the benefits of physical activity but provides exposure to natural sunlight—one of our sources for getting Vitamin D. "Low levels of Vitamin D are associated with risk of major depressive disorder and disturbances to the normal cycles of our body clock" (Selhub and Logan 2012, p.196). Take a walk barefoot and you get the benefits of "earthing" as well!

GET YOUR HANDS IN THE DIRT

It turns out that gardening has an added benefit of exposing us to healthy microbes in the soil. These microbes help to improve wellbeing: "Exposure to friendly soil bacteria could improve mood by boosting the immune system just as effectively as antidepressant drugs, a new study suggests" (LiveScience.com 2007). In addition,

Researchers from Bristol University and University College London discovered, using laboratory mice, that a "friendly" bacteria commonly found in soil activated brain cells to produce the brain chemical serotonin and altered the mice's behavior in a similar way to antidepressants. (Paddock 2007)

One way to encourage your children to get their hands in the earth's soil more often is to plant and care for gardens together. This is why an entire section is devoted to gardens in this book.

EAT LOCAL AND ORGANIC FOODS

Locally grown foods and organic foods cut down on the exposure to pesticides, food additives, and genetically modified organisms (GMOs). Grow your own food when feasible—many municipalities offer community gardens where people can grow and care for their own plants. You can also buy produce, eggs and other staples from farmers' markets and local farm stands, or shop at stores that stock and support organic foods.

Part I

NATURE IS THERAPEUTIC

Chapter 1

INCORPORATING NATURE IN YOUR THERAPEUTIC PRACTICE

As a counselor I find it puzzling that we are not educated, trained, supervised, or mentored to bridge more connections between our clientele and the natural world. There is plenty of data to back what many of us instinctively feel—that when we eat healthier, get fresh air and sunshine, exercise, and interact in the natural world we simply feel better.

In this section for professionals, I offer interventions that are nature based. I start with ways to bring nature to your office before treatment even begins. Many of us who work in the field of social work are office bound. Many social workers spend their working days in hospital wards, rehabilitation centers, classrooms, or other working environments which make it difficult to get outside with clients. If you can't get outdoors with your clients, there are still ways to bring the outdoors in.

I also delve into tasks that a social worker (or someone in a similar profession) might be expected to do, such as gather client data, complete an assessment, actively listen to the clients share their stories and life experiences, or address treatment goals. Within each of these areas I provide ways to add nature-based materials or nature-based activities to your work.

BRING NATURE INTO THE OFFICE

Regardless of your work space, there are ways to incorporate nature-based activities and materials in your work with clients. Start with your work space—bring as much nature into your office, hospital ward, desk, classroom, group home, and so on as you possibly can.

1. Decorate the walls with images of natural spaces that invoke a sense of awe, beauty, or relaxation. If your space is limited

or if you have other artwork you want on the walls, choose one section of the office to devote to nature and hang your nature-themed prints there.

2. Bring in several potted plants—they can help lower blood pressure, decrease anxiety and increase positive thoughts! Selhub and Logan note the following:

> Ulrich confirms that the mere presence of flowering and foliage plants inside a hospital room can make a difference. Specifically, in those recovering from an appendectomy and randomly assigned to a room with a dozen small potted plants, the use of pain medication was significantly lower than that of their counterparts in rooms with no potted plants; they also had lower blood pressure and heart rate, and rated their pain to be much lower. As well, those who had plants in their rooms had comparatively higher energy levels, more positive thoughts, and lower levels of anxiety. (Selhub and Logan 2012, p.23)

3. It is beneficial to have a window in your office. If the window looks out to a natural setting or has a view of trees and foliage, even better. "While the view can obviously enhance the mood and cognitive performance of employees, simply allowing sunshine into the interior space has been associated with increased job satisfaction, well being, and intent to stay with an organization" (Selhub and Logan 2012, p.96).

4. Keep collections of natural items on a shelf where clients can access them. These collections can be viewed for relaxation or they can be used for specific therapeutic activities. Refer to the nature-based collections on page 43 for further information.

5. Play relaxing music that has nature sounds in it. Sound machines, specific CDs and MP3s, and even iPod applications have nature-based songs and ensembles that include the sounds of ocean waves, frogs, singing birds, and more. These sounds can be soothing for some clients and used for white noise if needed.

6. Use guided imagery that incorporates exposure to the natural world. Guided imagery helps people quiet their minds and relax. There are two examples of guided imagery on pages 45–50.

7. Assign homework that encourages more fresh air, being outdoors, and connecting to the natural world. Refer to page 20 for examples of nature-based homework assignments you can assign clients.

8. Bring in a fish bowl or aquarium. Louv notes, "Research has shown that subjects experienced significant decreases in blood pressure simply by watching fish in an aquarium" (Louv 2008, p.45).

9. Bring in therapy animals if possible. Selhub and Logan state:

> Even the simplest act of petting a dog has shown to reduce physiological markers of stress reactivity and improve immune system function. Research using sophisticated electroencephalograph (EEG) readings has shown that interacting with therapy dogs brings about change in brain wave activity that are in line with states of mental relaxation. (Selhub and Logan 2012, pp.134–135)

> In addition they note, "A number of studies have shown that interacting with dogs can cause an increase in the production of oxytocin. Oxytocin, a hormone-like peptide produced by the brain, is in many ways the elixir of positive psychology" (Selhub and Logan 2012, p.134).

If you are a mental health worker who is mobile, without an office, or shares an office space, then bring one nature-based item with you to a session or shift when you can. Bring a plant, a jar of seashells, or even a nature-based photo book you think your client might like. All of these interventions remind your client of what is beautiful in the natural world and provides a connection to nature, even if it's a brief one. Get your clients interested, curious and intrigued about life outside of walls and screens.

HOMEWORK ASSIGNMENTS

Before our next session:

Take a 15-minute walk each day, rain or shine. ☐

Walk barefoot on the earth (non-paved areas) for 20 minutes a day when possible. ☐

Start a garden—indoors or outside. ☐

If confined to the indoors, find a sunny spot to sit in for a few minutes each day. ☐

Bring potted plants into your home or room. ☐

Spend time with animals and be kind to them. ☐

Explore a new natural space this week—a park, a trail, a swimming hole, a tree, and so on. ☐

Open your windows and let some fresh air in. ☐

Limit screen time to two hours a day. ☐

Eat healthier foods. ☐

Go outside and play for at least one hour a day. ☐

THE INITIAL APPOINTMENT

Initial appointments might include data collection, insurance and payment verification, or completing a client assessment. Social workers use this information to determine which services or treatment methods might be helpful to the client. Depending on your role with the client, it might be helpful to find out the following:

1. How many hours of screen time per day does the child get?

2. If the child does get screen time, where is the screen time coming from? Is it TV? Video games? Social networking sites online?

3. Is the content of the screen time age-appropriate?

4. Who, if anyone, is monitoring the content of what the child views on screen?

5. What does the child eat? Does the child eat a well-balanced diet of healthy foods?

6. How often does the child go outside and play? What does the child like to do outdoors?

7. Are there pets in the home? If so, how does the child treat the pet? How is the pet treated, in general, by the family?

Based on the answers to these questions you can start to build a picture of how the child spends their time during the day and where to make suggestions for ways they can improve their wellbeing.

Before I even consider a medication management referral, for example, I like to see if the child's wellbeing improves with less screen time, healthier foods, and more nature-based activity.

HELP CLIENTS TELL THEIR STORY WITH NATURE-BASED MATERIALS

The other part of completing an assessment is finding out what brought the client to you in the first place. Every client has a story—how they came to where they are at this moment, what they have experienced, and what has brought them joy and pain in their lives. This part of our work is incredibly important. Every person deserves to tell their story and be heard, whatever their age.

The following activities provide tools that help clients share their stories and help social workers complete the client assessment. Children are wonderful storytellers and will use props such as sand trays, doll houses, puppets, and figurines to act out and show what their lives have entailed. The uniqueness of the following activities is that they are made from nature-based materials. Clients often ask me where I find the toys and games that I have in my office and many of them are surprised to find out I went to a lake, beach, or into the woods to gather the supplies for the very "toys" and tools they love to play with.

STORYTELLING STONES

Storytelling Stones are a collection of stones that have varied characters and symbols on them. They can be used in a variety of therapeutic activities including sand tray therapy and storytelling games.

I have my own collection of Storytelling Stones that I made for my office, and I keep blank stones on hand so that clients can create pieces for their own story-sharing needs. The advantage of having clients create a few additional stones for their own therapy and story-sharing work is that 1) the client can customize pieces to enrich their storytelling details specific to their story and 2) the activity builds connection between the provider and client. As many of us have experienced, activities provide a comfortable way of engaging clients without the need for direct eye contact or making clients feel pressured to talk. Sometimes the act of co-creating art is a gentle way to build a therapeutic relationship.

There are three methods for creating these stones—painted, illustrated, and collaged. I will cover the directions for all three versions, but first and foremost you need to know what you want for characters and symbols for your storytelling collection.

Create a list of characters and objects you want to include in your collection. This will depend on the age group you work with, as well as culturally important pieces to include. I have created a list of possible pieces you may want to make. Its purpose is to show examples and provide some guidance on possibilities. Highlight the pieces you want to create and add extras based on the population of clients you work with.

CHARACTERS AND OBJECTS FOR STORYTELLING STONES

People:

- Nondescript adult males and females that could represent parents, school staff, and family friends.
- Nondescript male and female children who can represent friends and siblings.
- Rescue and medical staff (e.g. police officer, fire fighter, and doctor).
- Clergy, shaman, religious and spiritual leaders.
- Thief or robber.

- Person in jail clothes.
- Person in hospital clothes.

Archetypal and metaphorical characters:
• Wizard • Witch • Fairy godmother • Royalty • Grim Reaper • Ghost • Alien • Vampire • Superhero

Pets:
• Dog • Cat • Goldfish • Snake • Mouse • Hamster

Totem animals:
• Wolf • Owl • Turtle or tortoise • Crab • Crocodile
• Dragon • Hawk • Eagle • Fox • Deer • Dolphin • Frog
• Swan • Skunk • Spider • Rabbit • Raven • Coyote
• Dove • Bee • Ladybug • Cricket

Buildings and shelter:
• House • Apartment building • School • Places of worship
• Motel • Hospital • Camper van • Tent

Vehicles:
• School bus • Taxi • Ambulance • Police car • Fire truck
• Family car • Airplane • Boat • Pirate ship • Rocket ship
• Bicycle

Other:
• Flowers • Thundercloud • Rainbow • Moon • Heart
• Magic wand • Music note • Trophy • Bridge • Mountain
• Coin or money symbol • Skull and bones • Gun • Fire or explosions • Foreboding door

Words:
• Happy • Sad • Mad • Scared • Alone • Help • Love

Count up the number of characters and other objects you need from the lists above. It may help to add a few extra stones to your final number to allow for errors and last-minute additions.

Stones can be collected from places including the beach, riverbeds, quarries, stony desert areas, and other public spaces. If possible, include clients in the stone collection process. Clients can collect stones for their own pieces, while you collect stones for yours. Keep in mind you will be painting and drawing on these stones, so the smoother the better. An exception to this is when you find stones that create metaphorical pieces on their own—for example, a jagged black stone can be used in storytelling to represent something frightening that the child is not able or ready to put words to. It could also represent fear, anxiety, or depression. A large stone could represent an obstacle. A shiny or sparkly stone could represent a treasure or something magical.

At a pinch, stones can also be purchased from crafts stores and garden centers.

Figure 1.1 Painted, illustrated, and collaged versions of Storytelling Stones

Painted storytelling stones

Materials:

- Flat, smooth stones of various sizes.
- Acrylic paints.
- Paintbrushes with small tips.
- Toothpicks.
- Varnish.

Directions:

1. Rinse the stones and allow them to air dry.
2. Paint the stones with your characters, animals, and places. The toothpicks are helpful in adding small details such as eyes or letters. You can use multiple toothpicks or you can wipe off paint from the tip of the toothpick and re-use it.
3. Allow the paint to dry.
4. Apply a thin layer of varnish over the painted part of the stone.
5. Allow varnish to dry. Now your stones are complete!

Illustrated storytelling stones

Illustrated stones are simpler to create than painted stones because ink pens have a fine tip which allows for more ease and control of drawing. In addition, ink dries more quickly than paint.

Materials:

- Flat, smooth stones of various sizes.
- Permanent ink pens—if you are using dark-colored stones, use pens with white or light tones of ink; if using white stones, use pens with dark-toned ink.

Directions:

1. Rinse the stones and allow them to air dry.

2. Simply draw the images onto the stones with the pens.

3. Allow the ink to dry.

Collaged storytelling stones

Instead of drawing or painting directly onto the stones, images from magazines and books can be used for your pictures. Decoupage glue is used to seal the images onto the stones. The advantage of this activity is you can create beautiful storytelling stones without having any artistic talent whatsoever. Magazines can be helpful for finding words you need for your collection. Children's dictionaries and picture books are the easiest source for finding illustrations. Tag sales, yard sales, and second-hand shops usually have these types of books at very little cost.

Materials:

- Flat, smooth stones of various sizes.

- Scissors.

- Small pictures or words cut from magazines or books.

- Paintbrush.

- Decoupage glue.

Directions:

1. Rinse the stones and allow them to air dry.

2. Cut out the images and words you need from the books and magazines.

3. Use the paintbrush to apply a thin layer of decoupage glue to the underside of the image and then place the image on the stone. Smooth out any bumps.

4. Allow the image to dry on the stone.

5. Apply a thin layer of decoupage glue over the image and top of the stone. This will seal your picture onto the stone.

6. Allow to dry completely before using.

You can use the stones in a few different ways for storytelling purposes:

STORYTELLING STONES IN SAND TRAY WORK

The stones you made can be included with other figurines you already use in your sand tray work. They work the same as any piece you already use.

STORYTELLING STONES IN INDIVIDUAL AND GROUP WORK

Storytelling Stones can be used in individual as well as group storytelling activities. Clients choose stones from a bag and tell a story based on the stones they chose. You can create any mix of Storytelling Stones for the purpose of this activity (i.e. some stones can be painted, others collaged, and some may have words written on them). However, it is helpful to limit the number of stones in this activity so the bag is not too heavy. You can also try to limit the size of the stones to allow for a larger collection.

Materials:

- Collection of Storytelling Stones.
- Cloth bag for the stones.

Individual session

Ask the client to remove 3–5 stones from the bag without looking. Have the client tell you a story using the stones they chose.

Group session: Option 1—practice listening skills

This first option focuses on allowing each group member to tell a story. Have each person in the group take a turn using the Storytelling Stones just as they would if it were an individual session. One at a time, group members take a turn removing stones from the bag and tell a brief story based on the stones they chose. They then put their stones back in the bag and pass the bag to the next person in the group who takes their turn.

Discussion and reflection:

1. How do we know when someone is listening to us?

2. What are the challenges for you in listening to other people?

3. How can we become more present and engaged as listeners?

4. What is it like to be the one listened to?

5. How do you want people to listen to you?

6. Do you feel listened to in your life? Are there people who you wish would listen to you more?

7. What themes or emotion came through in the stories that people told?

8. Did you relate to any of the stories told? If so, how?

Group session: Option 2—group storytelling

One person starts by taking a Storytelling Stone from the bag, and then hands the bag to the next person. The bag gets passed around the circle or group until everyone has one stone. Then, the first person starts a story based on the stone they chose. You can set limits on how brief you want the story details to be (e.g. one or two sentences) based on the time you have for the activity. The next person adds a detail to the story based on the stone that they chose, and so on. Everyone in the group takes one turn. The last person in the group is responsible for bringing the story to a conclusion or end.

Discussion and reflection:

1. How does it feel to be part of the story and yet not have control over how it evolves or how it ends?

2. How is this type of storytelling like our own life stories?

EMOTION/EMOTICON STONES

Add pictures to individual stones of faces that show various feelings and facial expressions. You can paint the faces, illustrate them with ink, or use decoupage glue to seal images from magazines and books onto the stones.

If working with tweens or teens you can use the collage technique to use emoticons or words in place of feelings faces. Download a list of emoticon symbols from the internet or cut feelings words from magazines to collage onto the stones.

Keep the stones in a bowl or a bag and then have a client choose one.

Discussion and reflection:

- What feeling is being expressed here?

- Was there a time during the day or week when you felt the same way?

TALKING STICKS

Talking Sticks have been used in group and family work for many years. A Talking Stick is a stick that is used to represent who has the honor of speaking and being listened to in that moment. It is used to give a visual for group participants: the person who has the stick is talking, and the others are listening. When the person who has the Talking Stick is done saying what they need to say, they hand the stick back to the group facilitator who then hands it to the next person whose turn it is to speak. In this regard, a Talking Stick can be a tool for working with groups and families around communication and collaboration.

You can make your own Talking Sticks to use in your work with clients. They can be made from any type of stick but it is preferable to make sure it is free of insects, sharp points or splintery pieces, and is about the size of your forearm. You can certainly choose any size but I have found that larger sticks are distracting and smaller sticks can be hard to see for some group members.

Talking Sticks can be decorated or plain. Here are ideas for decorating your Talking Stick:

- Paint the Talking Stick in patterns or images. Acrylic paint works best for painting sticks.

- Tie a ribbon or two to the end of the stick. You can even attach beads and feathers to the ribbon.

- Use colored or metallic thumbtacks and press them into the stick in a pattern or design. This works best with thicker sticks.

- Wrap the Talking Stick in yarns or string. Tie off the yarn or string at the ends, looping the string through other layers to make sure it stays intact. You can also glue the ends in place.

Figure 1.2 Talking Sticks and Wishing Wands

WISHING WANDS

Children enjoy using Wishing Wands in their play as it gives them a tool for expressing their heart's desires as well as practice what it's like to have power. Wishing Wands also give professionals the opportunity to assess and address different clinical issues with clients. Here are some examples:

- Does the client make wishes about what they need for survival, such as "I wish my family had food," "I wish my family had a place to live," "I wish my home was safe"? These types of wishes may indicate the child is in survival mode and should be a red flag for professionals. In an ideal world the professional would assess the needs of the client and be able to refer the client to the appropriate services and resources, such as case management. Of course, we do not live in an ideal world, and more and more social service programs and services are being cut or reduced. However, if you are in a position to be able to assist your client in meeting basic needs, your client will be more able to engage in the clinical work.

• Professionals are used to hearing a general list of wishes (e.g. "I wish I had a million dollars," "I wish I had a pet unicorn," "I wish I could have all the ice cream in the world"). So it's easy to understand that there are some wishes that catch our attention. For example, "I wish I was a boy" (when the client is a girl), "I wish my grandfather would die," "I wish my little brother had never been born," "I wish I were dead." These types of wishes need more exploration. Sometimes a girl will wish she were a boy because she wants to play baseball and not feel pressured to play on a girl's softball team. But a girl may wish she were a boy because she is struggling with her gender identity (or she is fine with her gender identity but is struggling with others' discomfort with who she is). She may know and feel she is a boy, but feel "stuck" in a girl's body. In the same regard, a child who wishes his grandfather dead may know his grandfather is at the end of his life with a terminal illness and feel that the grandfather would be at peace if he died. But the child could also be wishing the grandfather would die because he has suffered a traumatic event at the hands of his grandfather. When clients make wishes that veer from the usual, explore the reasons as appropriate.

• Wishes can also expose the worries and fears of a child. If a child is given a pretend wish, for anything at all in the whole wide world, and their answer is "Mom won't get in a car crash today" or "I wish I could stop counting my steps," then you have an opportunity to explore this further with the client. Is this something they worry or think about a lot? If so, how often? To what degree are these worries or compulsions consuming the child's time?

- There are wonderful moments when children make wishes that show the amount of loving kindness they have. Some children are empathic and sensitive and might use a wish for someone else's benefit. However, if you work with a client who has trouble asserting their needs or who always ignores their own needs over others', then you can address this dynamic with the client in clinical work.

Painted wishing wands

Materials:

- A stick about a foot long that has no bark on it.
- Fine sandpaper.
- Acrylic paints.
- Paintbrushes.

Directions:

1. Wipe off any debris and dirt from the stick.

2. If there are jagged or rough spots on the stick you can use fine sandpaper to sand it down as smooth as you like. Some kids don't mind lumps and bumps, whereas other kids prefer a smoother wand. If you are making the wand for your own work, then it's best to err on the side of caution and make the wand with a smoother surface.

3. Paint the stick with patterns or designs—stars and moons, stripes, hearts, or polka dots are kid-friendly patterns if you are not sure what to paint.

Nature-based wishing wands

Nature-based Wishing Wands are magic wands made with natural materials.

Materials:

- A stick, with or without bark, about a foot long.
- Small- to medium-sized paintbrush.

- Decoupage glue.

- Nature-based decorations—pressed flowers, dried flowers, acorn caps, crystals, small flat stones, small leaves, and small feathers.

- Silver wire.

- Embroidery string or thin ribbon.

Directions:

1. Use the paintbrush to apply a thin layer of decoupage glue to the stick where you want to apply your pressed flower or leaf. Lay the flower or leaf over the decoupage glue and press down gently. Dip your paintbrush back in the decoupage glue and apply a thin layer of it over the flower or leaf. Repeat as necessary until you have applied all the pressed flowers or leaves you are using.

2. Allow the decoupage glue to dry thoroughly. You can lean the tip of your stick against an object to help it dry faster and more easily.

3. If you want to add crystals or stones to your wand, you will need to wrap them in wire first. This will take some patience as it takes a few tries to wrap the stone in place so that it won't slip off. Wrap and twist the ends of the wire around the wand where you want the stone to be.

4. Feathers and dried flowers can be tied onto the wand with embroidery string or thin ribbon.

NATURE-THEMED FAMILY PORTRAITS

One of my favorite assessment and drawing activities is asking clients to draw their family within a category or theme. Although the activity itself is not made from natural materials, it does help connect the client to thinking about their own identity with nature. This activity also helps children tell their story about the people they live with, where they came from, and how they define their own role in the family.

Whichever theme you choose, be flexible with the activity. Younger children, most likely, will not grasp the metaphorical references of this activity and therefore can opt to draw a picture of their family as they choose. Older youth, however, tend to enjoy this activity as it allows for creative thinking as well as artistic expression.

Materials:

- Paper.

- Markers or crayons.

- Pencils.

Directions:
Draw your family as if everyone in the family were an animal, tree, or body of water. Pick one theme and draw everyone you live with (or that is in your family) according to that theme.

Draw your family as animals

Many times a person's personality traits and characteristics will emulate one or more animals based on the same traits. With that in mind, think about the person's character and try to match them up to an animal with the same type of personality. Do this for each person in the picture. The following are examples only—feel free to reinterpret or create different metaphors based on your own knowledge base or experience.

- Nurturing and protective—a bear or elephant.

- Aloof, lazy, slow, or methodic—a sloth.

- Industrious and always on the go—an ant, bee, or hummingbird.

- Wise—an owl.

- Silly or playful—a monkey, puppy, dolphin, or otter.

- Quiet, relaxed and "Zen"—a praying mantis, panda bear, or whale.

- Aggressive or ready to attack—a crocodile or cobra.

- Sly—a fox or crow.

Draw your family as trees

You can replace the animal theme with trees and try out different characteristics with tree types. Draw a forest that represents your family.

- Strong and confident, family oriented—an oak tree.
- Flexible, patient—a willow tree.
- Finicky or difficult to nurture—a Japanese maple or bonsai tree.
- Friendly, bright, outgoing—a maple tree.
- Stands out from the crowd, likes to be noticed—a birch tree.
- Loyal, dependable—a pine tree.
- Perseveres, successful, looks over others—a redwood.
- Happy, content—a cypress tree.
- Life-giving, generous, nurturing, parental—a baobab ("the tree of life").
- Generous—a Christmas tree.

Draw your family as bodies of water

You can also draw your family as bodies of water. Draw the Earth or a map and then draw the bodies of water where they would fit. Some bodies of water might be closer to each other, some might be further apart.

- Strong-willed or powerful—an ocean.
- Slow moving and depressed, going nowhere—a mud puddle.
- Adventurous or wild—a white water river.
- Calm and reflective—a reflecting pool.
- Someone you don't trust—murky water, such as from a ditch or gutter.
- Playful and full of joy—a fountain or bubbling brook.

- Unpredictable, scary, and threatening—a water tornado, whirlpool, or tsunami.

- Healthy or nurturing person—hot springs or a natural spring.

- Cold, uncaring—ice or a glacier.

- Someone who respects you and loves you unconditionally—a water crystal.

Discussion and reflection:

1. What was it like to do this activity? Which parts were easy, and which parts were challenging?

2. How did you end up representing yourself?

3. How do you think other people in your family would have drawn you? Or each other?

4. What animal, tree, or body of water would you want to be, if you could choose?

WORRY DOLLS AND WISH DOLLS

There are two types of nature-based dolls that I make with clients—Worry Dolls and Wish Dolls. In both cases these dolls are made using natural materials such as sticks, clay, grasses, leaves, straw, acorns, and so on. The child writes a wish or a worry on a thin strip of paper and wraps it around the body of the doll before decorating it. Once decorated, no one sees the paper and therefore the child's worry or wish remains private.

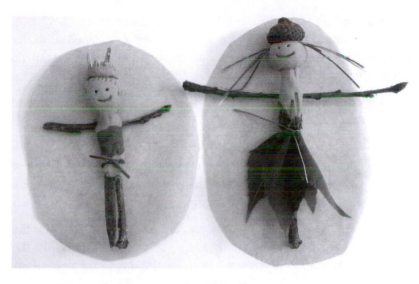

Figure 1.3 Examples of Worry and Wish Dolls

Materials:

- Small sticks of various sizes from 2–5 in (5–13 cm).

- String, thread, wire, or thin ribbons.

- Self-drying clay.

- Paper.

- Scissors.

- Pencil.

- Glue.

- Nature-based materials, such as grass, flowers, reeds, willow branches, acorn caps, leaves, and twigs.

Directions:

The following directions are for making a person-shaped doll, but if your client is making the wish doll for an animal, they can shape their doll into the animal figure.

1. Choose one larger stick for the body of the doll and one smaller stick for the arms.

2. Hold the smaller stick perpendicular to the body and then bind the sticks together by wrapping string diagonally around each side of the arms. The string will wrap around the body in an "x" formation. Tie the string once the arms are secured.

3. Form a ball out of the clay for the head. It helps to form the face after attaching the head to the body. Either sculpt the facial features or draw the face into the clay using a pencil tip.

4. Cut a thin strip of paper and write a wish or worry on it.

5. Wrap the paper around the body of the doll either above or below the arms. Glue it into place or use a piece of clay to secure it.

6. Use your nature-based materials to decorate and clothe the doll. Make sure clothing covers the strip of paper that the wish or worry is written on. Paper can also be used to create clothing if needed.

7. Allow the doll to dry.

Worry dolls

Many times, the kids I work with are worried about adult issues rather than age-appropriate issues (e.g. worrying mom will get into an argument with her boyfriend because mom went out with her friends last night and the child knows that the boyfriend gets jealous when mom spends time with friends). Other times, I work with kids who are chronic worriers. I use the Worry Dolls to help kids visualize putting their worries in "time out" for a while so they can focus on age-appropriate issues (e.g. who to play with at recess). The Worry Dolls "hold onto the worries" for the child so that the child can turn their attention to other things.

Wish dolls

I make Wish Dolls with young clients when a pet or loved one has died or the child is grieving for other reasons as these are helpful for children in the grieving process. The child makes a wish specifically for the person or pet that has passed away. For example, a child might wish the following: "My wish for Grandpa is that he gets all the root beer he wants in heaven" or "My wish for my dog is that she gets to swim as much as she wants now." Be sensitive to the child's religious, spiritual, and philosophical beliefs about death and/or life after death. If the child does not believe in life after death, they can use the wish doll in another way, such as "My wish for myself is that I can be as courageous as my grandfather was."

I also use Wish Dolls on occasions where it is appropriate for the child to make a wish, or express a hope or dream for themselves. In these circumstances I give the child some guidelines, such as "What could you wish for that would help you get through this phase in your life more easily?" Whether the situation is recovering from trauma, poverty, chronic or terminal illness, and so on, the child has an opportunity to think about and express what they need in order to feel more empowered to get through this experience. The Wish Doll holds onto that wish or dream as a reminder for the child to do so as well.

Wish Dolls are also wonderful tools for children who are grieving and struggling with situations such as national or international tragedies, relinquishing a pet to the shelter, when a classmate or teacher dies, when a family member far away becomes seriously injured or ill, and when they are worried about social and political issues such as climate change, the environment, and animal rights.

Wish Dolls give clients a venue for expressing what they wish they could give to someone else or what they would communicate to someone else if they had the opportunity, power, or ability to do so.

WISH BOOKS

Wish Books are art journals that kids create for the purpose of expressing their wishes and hopes. They are blank books that the client fills with pictures, photos, articles, words, poems, drawings, and so on that show and express what they wish for. This activity works well with children who are hospitalized, chronically ill, impoverished, homeless, or have little-to-no access to living their hopes and dreams at this moment. Wish Books are tools for expressing and communicating what the heart desires. The books can be a motivator and reminder that even when life is most challenging, there are still things to look forward to and strive for.

Wish Books can be created with various wishing themes. For the purpose of this activity I will focus on the theme "Nature Wish Book." This is a theme you can work on with your client to help find connections between them and the natural world.

Start by brainstorming places, animals, and natural phenomena your client would like to experience. Here is what a list might look like when it is completed and ready to put in a Nature Wish Book:

- I want to watch a meteor shower.

- I want to visit the desert and walk along the ridge of a giant sand dune.

- I want to climb a mountain.

- I want to swim in a hot spring.

- I want to go on a safari.

- I want to see the ocean.

- I want to catch fireflies.

- I want to go zip-lining in the rainforest.

- I want to have a picnic in the park.

- I want to hold a snake.

- I want to touch real snow.

- I want to see the Northern Lights.

- I want to climb a tree.

- I want to walk barefoot in the park.

Once your client has compiled a list, then you can gather your materials and start the Wish Book.

Materials:

- A blank book—this can be made by folding several pieces of paper in half and stapling the papers on the fold. Just make sure you have plenty of pages for all of your wishes.

- Markers, crayons, pens.

- Travel magazines, nature magazines, animal magazines (optional).

- Scissors.

- Glue.

Directions:

1. Write down one wish per page in your book.

2. If you have a picture of your wish, cut out the picture and glue it onto your wish page. The picture might be a photo someone gave you, it could be from a magazine, or printed from an online source.

3. If you do not have a picture, you can draw your own. Draw yourself doing what you wished for. If you do not like drawing directly in your book, draw it on another piece of paper and then cut it out and glue it into your book.

4. You can also write a few sentences about why you wish for this experience.

5. Leave a few blank pages so you can add to your book if needed.

If you are ever feeling down or as if life has nothing to offer you right now, look through your book. Imagine yourself on one of these adventures. Remember that the world has amazing places and things for you to experience.

Figure 1.4 Examples of a Wish Book and Nature-Themed Family Portraits

Chapter 2

RELAXATION AND MINDFULNESS

Relaxation and mindfulness are core skills we teach clients to help them manage life changes, anxiety, attention deficit, depression, impulsivity, and more. In a fast-paced world where people are inundated with multiple sources of stimulation, it's important to know how to quiet the mind and body for rest and rejuvenation.

If you are a professional "stuck" in the confines of an office, you can still include nature-based interventions to teach skills in relaxation and mindfulness. Here are some activities that can be done indoors.

INDOOR ACTIVITIES FOR PRACTICING RELAXATION AND MINDFULNESS

NATURE-BASED COLLECTIONS

Have you ever watched someone become mesmerized with a collection of objects? There is something soothing about looking through a plethora of items that are all similar and yet a little different. For this reason, I try to keep a couple of jars or small boxes of collected items in my office. Marbles, hardware goods (nuts, bolts, screws), gumball machine toys, and buttons have all been loved and picked over by my clients through the years. However, the nature-based collections of stones, sea glass, and seashells have been the most popular among the clients I've worked with.

Directions:

1. Collect various stones, shells, or sea glass with different shapes, patterns and sizes.

2. Rinse the items with water to remove dirt and debris.

3. Place the items on a towel or newspaper to dry thoroughly.

4. Inspect the items. Discard any pieces that may be too sharp.

5. Place in a suitable container such as a box or plastic container.

I use these collections for the following clinical purposes:

- Calming: Some clients enjoy sorting the objects as a calming activity. For example, one client might like to sort all the stones into colors. Another might like to sort them into shapes. Others might enjoy picking up the different stones and examining them. Sorting, holding, and observing can be calming for people of all ages.

- Sensory input: Other clients will enjoy the sensory input they receive from moving their hands through the objects. Stones can be soothing to run fingers and hands through. The stones themselves can be comforting to those who enjoy the feel of holding something weighted in their hand, or feeling the heat of their hands transfer to the stone. Shells have varied textures that are appealing to those who love the sensory input of ridges and bumps.

- Managing transitions: If your client becomes agitated or anxious about transitioning to or from your office, they may enjoy a few minutes at the beginning or end of session to look through a collection of nature-based items.

- Fidgets: Some people can focus better when their body is in motion or when they receive sensory input. In addition, for people who are uncomfortable with eye contact, it can be helpful for them to have something else to look at and fidget with. Keep a collection within reach so clients can use it if needed.

GUIDED IMAGERY

Guided Imagery is used in therapy to increase relaxation and wellbeing because it quiets the mind and helps the client practice visualization skills. You can read the following nature-inspired Guided Imagery stories to clients in sessions as a relaxation exercise.

GUIDED MEDITATIONS

The Forest—playing with fox pups

> Find a safe spot to get comfortable where you will still be able to hear my voice. [PAUSE].
>
> Take a deep breath to the count of three. [PAUSE].
>
> And breathe out. [PAUSE].
>
> Close your eyes and listen as I take you on a guided meditation to a forest where we will play with fox pups.

It is morning in the forest. Tall pine trees tower above the earth and all around you. The sun is peeking through the trees, making sunbeams all around. It is comforting to be surrounded by all these tall pines as you feel protected from the outside world and all of your worries.

You look down and see that the forest floor is covered with moss and pine needles so you take off your shoes and socks. It will feel so good to be barefoot in this forest. You walk over to a large tree. The ground is warm and soft beneath your feet. You put your hand out to touch the tree—the trunk is rough and bumpy. The bark smells like pine pitch—earthy and pungent. The bark is warm to the touch.

As your eyes scan the forest you notice a group of foxes huddled together taking a nap. One of the foxes lifts her head and she blinks her eyes in the sun. She then turns her head and she is looking right at you. She does not seem surprised or scared to see you. In fact, she looks curious.

You talk very quietly and gently to her. You ask her if it's okay to come closer to see the pups. She appears to be relaxed and friendly. The mama fox raises her head and then nods in your direction. "It is okay for you to play with my pups" is what she seems to say with that nod.

You call a fox pup over and she coyly approaches. She holds her head down as she comes closer to you. When she gets within reach, you hold your hand out for her to smell it. She takes in the scent of your hand and then steps closer to you. You pat her head gently and talk to her in a soothing, quiet voice. She seems to like this as she leans her head into your hand for more.

When the other pups see that you are friendly and kind, they shake off their sleepiness and walk over to see you. You introduce yourself to each of them in the same way, letting them smell your hand and then patting their heads and ears. You let each of them know you mean them no harm. As much as you'd like to wrap your arms around them and give them big hugs you know this might frighten them, so you continue to speak to them softly while patting them.

Take a moment to imagine how soft and warm the fox's fur feels in your hands. [PAUSE].

The first fox pup, the girl fox, seems to be feeling playful. She is nudging your hand and nodding her head toward a clearing in the trees. You and the other fox pups follow her to this spot where sunbeams are cascading down between all the pine trees and illuminating the dust particles in the air. The air feels energizing. As soon as the girl fox reaches this clearing she starts to run in tight circles, full of joy. The other pups start to chase her. The fox pups are scampering about and chasing each other around in circles. It looks like so much fun you decide to join in.

You jump into the circle of foxes. They are delighted you have joined in their play. They run around and around you. You feel a little dizzy watching them, but you are having so much fun you don't mind.

One of the foxes beckons you to chase her around the circle. You start to run after her, laughing so hard your knees feel weak. Your bare feet feel so light against the warm pine needles on the ground. Your heels kick up pine needles as you run. The foxes then tumble into each other and knock you over. You land softly on the soft carpet of pine needles, laughing even harder. The fox pups are panting. They've become tired but they are overcome with joy. They had never played with a human before and they are full of gratitude for the positive experience. You feel full of gratitude as well.

The mama fox has awoken from her nap and she nods at you again. It's as if she is saying, "Thank you for playing with my pups. I needed the rest." She makes a yip noise and all the pups go to her. It is time for them to continue with their responsibilities. And it is time for you to leave as well.

You picture your heart full of light and love for these foxes. You picture sending that light and love to each and all of them, surrounding them with beautiful white light and love.

In return, the foxes give you a message—you can hear it clearly in your head as if they had spoken it out loud: "Thank you for being gentle and playing with us."

You watch the foxes walk deeper into the forest as they leave. You say "goodbye" and feel the love and gratitude they are sending you as they depart. Then you look around, wondering where you left your shoes. Oh, there they are—right under the giant pine tree. You gather up your shoes and turn to face the path you walked in on.

It is now time to return to this world. [PAUSE].

Take a deep breath to the count of three. [PAUSE].

Now breathe out and slowly open your eyes when you are ready.

The Ocean—swimming with dolphins

Find a safe spot to get comfortable where you will still be able to hear my voice. [PAUSE].

Take a deep breath to the count of three. [PAUSE].

Now breathe out. [PAUSE].

Close your eyes and listen as I take you on a guided meditation where we will swim in the ocean with dolphin friends.

It is beautiful out on the ocean today. You have sailed your boat to these crystal blue waters to watch the sun set and to visit your dolphin friends. The dolphins love to pass between these islands at dusk. You know this because you have anchored your boat here many times before.

You bring your boat to a gentle stop. The boat rocks gently back and forth as you lift up the anchor on the deck and drop it into the water. The anchor is heavy and falls to the bottom of the ocean, where it sinks into the sand and holds the boat in place. [PAUSE].

Now that the boat is anchored you look all around you and take in the view. There are seven islands all around, each one surrounded by white sandy beaches and lush tropical trees and flowers. If you concentrate—if you focus your energy enough—you can even smell the flowers. They smell wonderful to you.

There are not many clouds in the sky at the moment and the sun is sitting low on the horizon. You scan the waters around the islands, looking for any sign of your dolphin friends. As you watch for them, you take off your shorts and shirt so that you are in your bathing suit, ready for a swim. You put your hand in the water to feel the temperature. The water has been soaking up the warmth of the sun all day and it feels perfectly warm and cool at the same time.

Slowly, you notice a feeling, a knowing, that the dolphins are near. You look around and see a dolphin pod off in the distance. The dolphins are leaping and splashing in the turquoise waters and they are heading your way.

You feel anticipation. The dolphins are very dear to your heart and they bring you so much joy. You are excited you will be swimming with them soon.

You climb up onto the side of the boat and balance yourself there for a moment. When you feel steady, you take a deep breath and dive head first into the crystal blue ocean. The water rushes through your hair, tickling your scalp. The water cascades over your shoulders, up your back, and all around your legs as you submerge. You feel as one with the ocean, invigorated by its energy. Now you stretch your arms and swim toward the dolphins. Even from this distance you can hear them under the waves, clicking and chattering to each other. It fills your heart with joy.

When you come up for a breath of air you can see the dolphins are only a short swim away. You take in another breath of air and dive back into the water. You swim for a few strokes and then you see the first of the dolphins! It smiles at you as if to say hello. Then more dolphins come into view. At last you are joined with your beloved dolphin friends.

The dolphins are friendly and full of love. They let you pat their sleek fins and long noses. You love how smooth they feel under your hands.

It is time for you to get another breath of air so you start to swim to the surface. A dolphin swims right beside you and beckons you toward her back fin. You reach out and hold onto her fin.

She pulls you up to the surface of the water and she floats there with you for a moment while you catch your breath. She is patient and she will wait for you to let her know when you are ready to play. [PAUSE].

Take in this moment. You are surrounded by beauty and love. You are accepted here for who you are. You are cherished. You are supported. [PAUSE].

You take in another deep breath. You hold onto the dolphin's fin firmly, but not too hard.

You gently tap the dolphin's side and she dives down into the water, pulling you with her. You can feel the grace and speed with which dolphins can move in the water. The dolphin's tail is moving quickly, propelling you and her through the waves. Some of the dolphins swimming next to you turn their heads to smile at you. This is a signal that you are all about to breach the water. You have been anticipating this moment.

The dolphin pulls you upward. You can see the surface of the water just above you. You can even see the wavy reflection of the sky on the water's surface. You are pulled closer and closer to it until—SPLASH—the dolphin and you leap right out of the ocean, into the fresh tropical air, and then back down into the water. If you weren't underwater at this moment, you would be laughing with joy—that was so much fun! The other dolphins have re-entered the water as well and they are all smiling as they swim. Everyone is having fun swimming and playing.

You are still holding onto your dolphin's fin and you give her another tap. She knows this means you want to do this again. She speeds up her swimming to gather momentum and then veers upward toward the water's surface. You hold tight as she pulls both of you right out of the water, up into the clear blue air, and then back down into the water with another splash. The other dolphins have followed.

You are having so much fun with these playful animals. But you can see by looking up at the water's surface that the sun is starting to sit low on the horizon. The water's surface is starting to shimmer in gold and yellow. It is time for you to go. You tap the dolphin twice and she knows it's time for you to go back. She will take you to your boat.

The dolphin changes direction as she knows exactly where your boat is. You are still holding onto her fin and she pulls you gracefully through the water, the entire pod swimming right next to you and her. Through the crystal-clear blue water you see the chain of the anchor swaying with the movement of the water. You have returned to your boat. You thank the dolphins from your heart. They nod at you with their smiling dolphin faces. You feel them return the positive energy—your heart suddenly feels lighter and full of nurturing love. You tell them, in your mind, that you will be back to swim with them soon, and they seem to understand as they nod one more time before swimming away.

You swim upward to the surface of the water and take in a long, deep breath. It is always an amazing experience to swim with the dolphins.

You climb onto your boat and then balance yourself on the deck. It takes a moment to get the feel of your legs again. As you take a moment to catch your breath, find your balance, and dry off, you watch the dolphin pod as it swims away toward the setting sun. Sunrise is your cue to pull up the anchor and head back home. You wave to the dolphins and feel their love in your heart. You will come back here soon. You will swim and play with them again. In fact, anytime you need to feel love, nurturing, and acceptance, just close your eyes and imagine swimming with your dolphin friends. They are always right here in your heart.

> Take a moment to breathe in and breathe out as we prepare for you to come back to the room. [PAUSE].
>
> Take in a breath to the count of three.
>
> Exhale—let your breath out to the count of three.
>
> And slowly open your eyes.

NATURE MOBILES

Mobiles can be calming because they provide an object in motion that is relaxing yet engaging to look at. If the child needs a few moments to self-soothe and calm down, then a mobile can be a relaxing focal point while taking deep breaths. Therefore, a Nature Mobile is a nice addition to your office or working space.

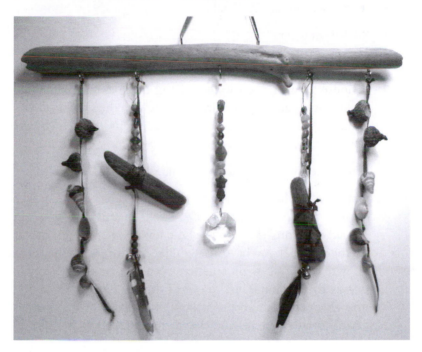

Figure 2.1 Example of a Nature Mobile

You can also help a client make a mobile for their own room or home. If possible, take a walk with your client and gather durable natural materials that can be added to the mobile—sticks, small- to medium-sized stones, shells, dried leaves, feathers, acorns, sea glass, and shells are all examples of materials that hang well on mobiles. You could also assign homework for the week in the form of a walk that your client takes with an adult in order to gather these materials for the next session.

Materials:

- Nature-based objects, such as twigs, dried leaves, acorns, shells, small stones or crystals, feathers, a prism.

- Beads (optional).

- One stick, about a foot (30 cm) long.

- Twine or string.

- Wire.

- Eye screw hooks (optional).

- Self-drying clay.

Directions:

1. Choose the items you want to hang from your mobile. Line the items up under your stick to make sure they will fit—you will need to leave at least a finger space between each vertical row.

2. Cut pieces of twine or string to hang from the mobile.

3. Attach your objects to the strings. Some of your objects might have a hole in them, such as a shell. In this case you can thread the string through the hole and tie a knot to secure it to the string. If you have an item like a stone, wrap the stone in wire first. This might take some practice, or more than one try, as the stone might slip out of the wire at first. Then tie the wrapped stone to the string. To attach shells and other "hard-to-attach" items, use clay to secure items to the string.

4. Now that all of your items are attached to string, tie the strings to the stick.

5. If you prefer to use eye hooks, screw the eye hooks into the stick. Then tie your strings to the eye hooks.

6. Finally, attach a string to the top of the mobile so you can hang it up.

DREAM CATCHERS

Dream Catchers are based on Native American tradition where a handmade web is adorned with nature-based items such as feathers and shells. The Dream Catchers are hung above a child's bed to capture bad dreams. If you work with a child who is scared of the dark, has trouble sleeping, or has unsettling dreams, then a Dream Catcher can be comforting for the child to have in their room.

Materials:

- A pliable tree branch (e.g. a willow tree branch).
- Twine or string.
- Scissors.
- Natural objects, such as feathers, shells, or crystals.
- Self-drying clay or wire.

Directions:

1. Bend and mold your tree branch into a circle shape.

2. Use string or twine to wrap the branch ends in place. Secure with a knot.

3. Cut an arm's-length piece of twine or string.

4. Tie one end of the twine or string onto the Dream Catcher.

5. Loop the string loosely around the perimeter, about every inch (2.5 cm), until you get back to the starting point.

6. Continue to make the next layer of loose loops—pull your string through each of the loops you just created.

7. If you have any items you want to add to the actual web, tie them on as you go.

8. Continue pulling the string through the string loops until you get to the center of the web. Tie the end of the string into place and then trim the excess string as needed.

9. Cut three pieces of string to hang from your Dream Catcher.

10. Attach the natural objects to the string. You can attach the objects with clay, string, or wire.

11. Tie the decorated strings onto the bottom of your Dream Catcher.

12. Tie a loop of string to the top of your Dream Catcher as a hanger.

Figure 2.2 Dream Catcher

NATURE COLLAGES

One project my clients ask to do over and over is making Nature Collages. The kids find and cut pictures of animals, sunsets, roses, gardens, and other nature-based images from various recycled magazines I bring in. The magazines might be about travel, backyard birds, gardening, or animals, or they may even be seed catalogues. The kids then glue their images onto a piece of construction paper.

When they have compiled their collage we discuss how they feel when they look at their own collection of pictures. Many times they use words and phrases like "relaxed," "calm," "like I want to go to those places," or "I feel quiet inside." I encourage the kids to use their collages as tools for practicing and using their visualization skills.

Discussion and reflection:

1. Choose one picture from your collage to focus on. Take a few moments to imagine yourself in that picture.

2. What would it feel like to be in that picture?

ANIMAL TOTEM SHRINES

In this activity you and a client transform a matchbox into an Animal Totem Shrine for the client. An animal totem is an animal that represents a lesson or a gift a person receives to help them through a situation or a lifetime. For example, a child who is learning to listen better might choose an animal that hears well for their animal totem. The shrine is a tool to remind your client of a goal they are working on. It can also be used for support and guidance. The shrine is small enough to fit in a purse or side pocket, which makes it portable, or it can be put on a shelf where the client will see it often.

Materials:

- Matchbox with a slide-out tray.

- Decorative papers.

- Scissors.

- Glue.

- Image of the animal—it can be a drawing, a sticker, or a picture cut out from a magazine or old book.

- Various trinkets and tokens to go in the shrine—can include small crystals, words that have been cut out from magazines or books, words drawn onto small stones, charms, beads, or other small, meaningful objects.

Directions:

1. Place the matchbox at the edge of one of the decorative papers and mark the width of the box. Then cut a strip of paper to that width.

2. Wrap the paper around the outside of the box—you can trim it as needed. Glue it into place.

3. Add a second, thinner strip of decorative paper if you like, for an added layer of color.

4. Glue the image of the animal to the outside of the matchbox, centered on the strip of paper.

5. Cut a small rectangle of paper to glue onto the floor of the matchbox tray.

6. Add items to the shrine as desired. Make sure they all fit into the tray of the matchbox and slide in and out easily.

7. Place your Animal Totem Shrine someplace special or bring it with you when you need a reminder of the goals you are working on.

Discussion and reflection:

1. Explore whether or not your client already has a connection to an animal or animals.

2. Is there an animal that shows up a lot in the client's life?

3. Is there an animal that has a trait your client wishes they had?

4. Does the client have a favorite animal? What is a strength or skill the animal possesses that your client could use to succeed in meeting their treatment goals?

Choosing totem animals for specific treatments

Below are some possible considerations of animal totems as they relate to specific treatment goals.

Speaking up and assertion

- Whippoorwill: I know from experience how vocal and persistent these birds are because a couple of them nest in our woods each summer. They call back and forth to each other all night and there is no ignoring them.

- Songbirds: They speak their voice through song.

- Lions and tigers: They use their powerful voices to roar.

- Monkeys: Various breeds of monkeys are quite vocal when they want to express something.

Learning to listen to intuition and trust self

Water animals, and animals that gather near water, are a nice match for clients who are getting re-familiarized with their intuition or awakening their intuition. Water is symbolic of listening to your inner feelings and thoughts. They include the following:

- Dragonflies.

- Salamanders.

- Frogs.

- Fish.

- Whales and dolphins.

Calming and relaxing

- Cats: Children who have cats for pets will relate to how relaxed a cat looks when it is lying in a sunbeam or stretched out for a nap.

- Praying mantis: These insects look as if they are praying. They are also slow moving and have an air of tranquility.

- Koala bear: Koala bears have a calm demeanor and love to rest.

- Sloth: These animals tend to move very slowly and deliberately, taking their time.

Acting your age (for children)

- Panda bears: The playful and calm personality of panda bears is appealing to children. Pandas can be a wonderful totem animal for children who need to slow down, relax, and take their time growing up.

Adapting to changes or transitions

There are many animals that go through major transformations and thrive in this world, in spite of adversity. Animals such as these are wonderful reminders that sometimes we have to think outside the box and find creative ways to survive. If your client is facing challenging circumstances and/or struggling to adapt, then one of these animals might be a reminder for them to try new and healthy ways to face the challenges facing them.

- Snakes: A snake might be an appropriate totem animal for a teen who is moving on to college or leaving home for the first time, because snakes must leave their old skin (home) in order to thrive.

- Hermit crabs: Hermit crabs have to find their shells and are used to moving from one shell to another. In this regard, hermit crabs are wonderful totems for children in foster care or for kids moving to a new home. They can also be used with children whose parents have divorced, when the child is adjusting to an additional home.

- Caterpillars: Caterpillars are useful totem animals when the child is facing hardship and life challenges. If a child is facing poverty, worried about a loved one with an addiction, witnessing or experiencing domestic violence, or has other external stressors, the caterpillar can be a supportive reminder that childhood in and of itself is temporary, and many times challenging. However, with patience and hard work the caterpillar transforms into a butterfly and has the freedom to decide where it wants to go.

- Chameleons: Chameleons are appropriate animal totems for children adapting to living in two households (e.g. in the case of separated or divorced parents). Chameleons change color based on their surroundings—much like people change their behaviors, based on their surroundings. Sometimes after a divorce or separation, children struggle with rules and expectations being different at one parent's house from the other. If the child can embrace chameleon power, they will learn to accept that one environment is different from the other and they can adapt to both.

Increasing self-esteem and self-worth

• Peacocks are a symbol of beauty and pride. Their feathers fan out in an elaborate display of blues and greens and gold. People buy peacock feathers simply for their beauty. It is no surprise that many people associate peacocks with pride and self-esteem.

• Lions are also associated with pride, as well as courage.

Sobriety

Anyone working with clients struggling with substance abuse or addictive behaviors knows that perseverance is the key to sobriety and breaking free of unhealthy patterns. Relapses happen and the road to recovery takes persistence to keep dusting off and to try again. If your client is challenged by these same issues, they may want to choose an animal totem that is also persistent.

• Squirrels: Squirrels are clever and persistent. People go to great lengths to keep them out of bird feeders—invention after invention has been created just to outsmart the persistent squirrel. It seems no matter how many obstacles get between the squirrel and the feeder, the squirrel finds a way to succeed.

• Wolves: Wolves can be good totems for people struggling with addictions, because the wolf pack is social and sticks together. A wolf totem reminds your client to reach out for support and to use their sponsor in the journey to sobriety. A sponsor is a person in Alcoholics Anonymous or other recovery group who has been sober, and who mentors another member of the group who is recently sober.

Stress relief and playfulness

Laughter and play are good for the soul and body. Our clients, even the youngest ones, can be so busy with school and extracurricular activities that they forget to just relax and have some down time. Other times we have clients who are so used to being "adultified" that they have become uncomfortable doing age-appropriate things like being silly, having tea parties, or playing "make believe." Here are some playful animals that are great totems for these kids who can benefit from more play:

- Otters.

- Seals.

- Dolphins.

- Puppies and kittens.

- Bear cubs.

Needing to feel nurtured and loved

There are many nurturing animals that are protective as well as loving with their young. If you work with a child who needs some parenting or nurturing, then one of these animals might be a good totem match:

- Whales.

- Dogs.

- Elephants.

Trying new things

Animals that leap or plunge are great totem animals for children who are afraid or anxious to try new things.

- Grasshoppers.

- Frogs.

- Flying squirrels.

Figure 2.3 Sorting objects to put in Animal Totem Shrines

PORTABLE ZEN GARDEN

Zen Gardens are simple gardens of sand and stone that typically evoke a sense of calm and relaxation. They can be used with clients to practice skills in mindfulness or used as a "fidget." You can keep a Portable Zen Garden in your work space and allow clients to create designs in the sand and rearrange the stones. Although kids of all ages enjoy the traditional "fidgets" many social workers have on their desks and tables, teens will appreciate the more sophisticated and mature appeal of a Zen Garden—it still allows them to fidget and doodle with the tools in the sand.

Of note: If you are going to use a Portable Zen Garden with children who are hospitalized due to chronic or terminal illness, make sure you follow guidelines for exposure—you may need to take additional care of your garden by keeping it covered between sessions (to keep dust out of it) or changing the sand and cleaning the tray, tools, and stones for each client.

Figure 2.4 A Portable Zen Garden

Materials:

- Clean, disinfected sand (this can be purchased from a hardware store).

- Pan or tray with sides at least 1 in (2.5 cm) in height.

- Fork, dowel, skewer, and other items that can serve as "tools" to make designs in the sand.

- Three to five smooth stones—the number and size of the stones will depend on the size of your Portable Zen Garden, so use your discretion.

Directions:

1. Add a layer of sand about ½ in (1 cm) thick to your pan or tray.

2. Use your "tools" to create patterns or designs in the sand such as a flowing or circuitous path through the garden.

3. Place stones in the garden where you like.

PORTABLE GREEN GARDENS

If you work in a hospital or institution, you can create a Portable Green Garden that is grown in a wagon. The garden is easily transported from room to room and can go outside for sunshine when needed (i.e. if there is not a sunny space in the building). You can plant flowers, grass, or even succulents in the wagon.

Depending on the client population, the wagon can be wheeled around for various activities, such as allowing kids to touch and smell the plants, plant flowers, pick flowers, put their feet in the grass, or use the garden as a landscape for a toy or figurines. Finally, the wagon can be used for rituals, such as graduations and going home. The child could plant a flower in the wagon as part of saying goodbye.

OUTDOOR ACTIVITIES FOR PRACTICING RELAXATION AND MINDFULNESS

ALPHABET TREES

There are times when focusing on the smaller details of an object is helpful for slowing down the mind and body. It is a practice in mindfulness—the more you bring your attention to the finer details of an object, the less you get lost or caught up in the chaos of everything else going on around you. I have used Alphabet Trees with children who are struggling with distraction and anxiety as a way to introduce them to practicing mindfulness. I ask older children to rate their level of anxiety or distraction before we start the activity so that we have a number to work with: "On a scale of 1–5 (1 = feeling calm and relaxed, 5 = panic attack), how would you rate your level of anxiety right now?" Then we go outside and find a tree with many branches. I ask the child to find as many of the letters of the alphabet as they can. Depending on the child's attention span you can ask the child to find the letters in their name or find only 10 letters, half the alphabet, or even the full alphabet—adjust the activity accordingly. When the activity is over or the child seems to have had enough, check in and see what number they would assign their level of anxiety at this point. Has it improved any? Whether the number goes up, down, or stays the same, it's okay. These numbers simply help you and the child figure out whether the intervention was a helpful one in using mindfulness to calm the mind.

You can also combine this activity with teaching reframing skills. Looking for alphabet letters in the trees sets the tone for conversation about looking at something through a different lens—in this case, looking beyond the tree itself to find alphabet letters.

DANDELION PUFFS

When dandelions "go to seed" they turn from plump, yellow flowers to wispy, ghostly-white puffs. You can blow the dandelion seeds off of the stem and watch them float in the breeze. Dandelions are abundant in some parts of the world, such as the United States. They typically show up in spring, and bloom and go to seed throughout the summer into fall. If dandelions do not grow near you, there may be a similar type of flower or plant that goes to seed in the same way dandelions do.

This simple activity can be used in a few ways in your work with clients.

- Assessment: You can use this activity as a wish-making activity. Some people make a wish before blowing the white seeds from a dandelion. (You can refer to Wish Dolls on page 38 to view the clinical aspect of wish-making in assessment work.)

- Mindfulness: Blow the seeds from a dandelion and have your client follow one dandelion seed with their eye as far as they can. Discuss whether the act of following the seed is challenging or not. For example, did the client get distracted or were they able to actually follow the seed's path?

- Managing change: You can do this activity with follow-up discussion about the seed's journey. If your client were the seed, what would it be like to be pulled from the flower and then carried on the breeze to a new location? What is it like to have no control? What is it like to experience new places?

What will the seed need in order to grow into a flower? Metaphorically, how is the life cycle of a flower similar to that of a person?

LABYRINTHS AND WALKING MEDITATIONS

One of my favorite activities to do with clients is to create and walk in labyrinths. Labyrinths look like a cross between a spiral and a maze, depending on the design. There are several labyrinth styles—from classical, traditional designs to modern, whimsical ones. Regardless of the design, labyrinths share certain characteristics, such as having one continuous (and often circuitous) path to the center. When you get to the center of a labyrinth, you turn around and exit the same way you came in. There are no blocks or tricks in finding your way to the center and back.

Labyrinths can be used for walking meditations, prayer, reflection, rituals, and healing.

Larger, more intricate labyrinths can feel overwhelming for young children because the pathways tend to be narrow and confined, which can lead to the temptation to jump over the boundaries. A three-circuit labyrinth is typically easier for children because it is a brief walk to the center and back, and the path tends to be wider. Wide pathways are also needed for wheelchair accessibility.

Try drawing your own three-circuit labyrinth.

Once you get the feel for drawing labyrinths on paper, try drawing them in an outdoor setting. If you are able to bring clients to the beach, sand is a wonderful medium for drawing labyrinths. If your office has a paved parking lot, consider drawing one in chalk (as long as it is a low-traffic, safe area to use).

There are additional activities you can do with permanent labyrinths if you have permission from the owner to do so: If the labyrinth pathway or boundary is made of paving or stepping stones, allow children to draw pictures and words in chalk, expressing their hopes and dreams. They can also write messages for loved ones who have passed away. In addition, candlelit labyrinths can be walked at night by setting tea lights along the path. A candlelit labyrinth can be walked in memory of someone special or simply for the beauty of it. As always, supervise children around candles.

Figure 2.5 Steps in drawing a three-circuit labyrinth

Figure 2.6 Following the path of a labyrinth in the sand

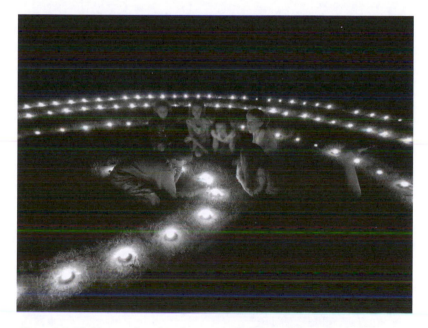

Figure 2.7 Children gathered in the center of a labyrinth lit with candles

STONE STACKING

Bring a client to an outdoor area where there are pebbles and stones, and challenge them to create a tower out of them. Stone stacking requires concentration and body control. The child naturally has to slow down in order to balance these stones on top of each other. For safety reasons set a rule that the child does not stack stones higher than their hips. After the activity you can have a discussion.

Figure 2.8 A stack of stones

Discussion and reflection:

1. What happens if you rush in and start putting stones on top of each other?

2. Have you ever rushed into a decision or project without planning ahead first? What was the outcome of rushing into that situation? Did you have to go back and re-do any part of it or make amends to anyone?

3. What happens when you slow down and take your time stacking stones? Does it make stacking the stones any easier?

4. Tell me about a time you planned ahead for a situation. What was that like for you to plan ahead? What was the outcome of planning ahead?

5. Was there any aspect of this activity that felt calming to you? If so, tell me what felt calming.

LIQUID SAND SCULPTURES

These mini sculptures with their irregular-shaped peaks remind me of stalagmites. It helps to use sand directly out of a tide pool or other sandy area where clean water has collected. The sand needs to be saturated with water to the point that it is almost liquid.

Directions:

1. Put your hand into the wet sand and pull out a handful, with your fingertips touching.

2. Let the wet sand fall through your fingertips. The sand will start to make a cone shape.

3. Keep adding sand to the cone until it is the desired height.

4. Repeat to make several towers.

5. At times the towers will collapse which is normal and just part of the process. You can always add a new tower if one collapses.

Watery sand towers can be a soothing activity for children who need sensory input, enjoy repetitive motion, or need something to fidget with in order to settle their bodies. They can also be created just for fun, as these boys are doing in Figure 2.9.

Figure 2.9 Making Liquid Sand Sculptures

PAINTING STONES WITH WATER

This activity can be used with clients who are grieving or struggling with impermanence and change.

All you need for this are stones (any size), a clean paintbrush and water. Fresh water or saltwater is fine and this activity can be done indoors or out.

Have the client try "painting with water." The client wets the paintbrush and then paints on a stone with the water. Designs, patterns, words, and pictures can be painted. Depending on the heat and humidity of your surroundings, the water will evaporate and dry from the stone, erasing the "painting."

Discussion and reflection:

1. Do you like how the water evaporates, erasing your picture? Or do you wish the image you created would last longer?

2. What is something in your life you wish had lasted longer?

3. What is something in your life you wish had disappeared or gone away sooner?

4. How are moments and life experiences like painting stones with water?

5. How does the expression "Be in the moment" relate to this activity?

MINDFULNESS IN NATURAL SPACES

Mindfulness is a skill and a practice that works well in natural spaces. Regardless of the setting (a beach, a grassy spot, a basketball court, a bench in the park, etc.) take a deep breath, hone in to the surroundings, and observe. Encourage the client to use all their senses to experience the moment. The moment could be one of the following:

- Wading in a fountain, puddle, pond, lake, or ocean.

- Burying feet in the sand or rocks.

- Holding rocks of various size and texture.

- Walking barefoot in the grass.

- Watching clouds pass by and change shape.

- Lying on rocks or boulders that have been warming in the sun.

Regardless of the setting, you may need to guide the client through the practice the first few times so they get an idea of how to view these experiences through a "mindfulness lens." Cue them into the moment and the practice. Below is a sample guide for talking the client through the experience. Choose some or all of the questions to ask during the exercise and pause between questions.

- What noises do you hear?

- Are there any noises that sound like they are coming from far away? Are there any noises that sound unfamiliar to you? What noises, if any, sound pleasing or comforting to you?

- Can you hear any movement in the air, such as a breeze blowing through leaves? Do you hear any birds? If so, listen and see if you can tell how many different types of birds are singing or calling.

- Do you hear any vehicles? If so, can you tell the sound of smaller vehicles from the sound of larger ones? Are there any noises that make you curious?

- What about smell—what scents do you smell?

- Which scents smell natural, such as trees or grass? Are there any scents here that smell toxic or bad? Are there any familiar smells here? Can you smell any dirt or dust here? Can you smell any perfumes? Does the air here smell warm or cold to you? Does it smell like it has rained here recently? Or does it smell dry?

- What can you feel at this moment?

- See if you can feel your feet. Focus on the feel of your feet against the water/grass/pavement etc. here. Can you feel the earth beneath your feet? Do you feel your connection to the earth? How do your legs feel? Your back? Your shoulders? Your neck? Are your muscles feeling relaxed in any part of your body? Are they feeling tense in any part of your body? Do you have any pain in your body—if so, where is the pain? Are you clenching or tightening any muscles? Is your tongue on the roof or bottom of your mouth? Where can you feel love in your body at this moment? How warm or cool is the air against your skin? Can you feel the clothes you are wearing against your skin?

- What do you see here?

- What movements, patterns, or objects are catching your eye at this moment? Is the surrounding area filled with any haze, sunlight, shadows, or darkness? Do you see any colors you like? How do your eyes feel as you look around? Do they feel tired or alert? Can you feel your pupils dilate if you close and open your eyes?

- Take a few deep breaths, in and out slowly to the count of three and then we will talk about what this was like for you.

After this exercise, discuss what it was like to be in the moment and tune in to the surroundings.

Chapter 3

SELF-ESTEEM AND POSITIVE CONNECTIONS

Many times we work with clients who have low self-esteem or low self-worth. And sometimes our clients have difficulty forging positive relationships with others. Nature provides a wonderful environment for children to work on connection to self and others.

MESSAGE STONES

Message Stones are smooth stones that have power words, mantra words, or positive messages painted on them. You can use these stones in a few different ways:

- Keep them in a bowl in your office. Clients can pick a stone out of the bowl and see what the message is. The stone's message can be used as a mantra for the day or until the next session. You could also ask the client to tell you a way the word applies to their life at the moment.

- Assign a Message Stone to the client if they are responsible enough to bring it back next session. This may be especially helpful when clients are going through a rough experience and need the added support of a transitional object to comfort them. For example, if a client is starting a new sobriety program that week, you could assign the stone "persistence," "strength," or "I believe in you." They could use this stone as a reminder that they are supported.

- Make Message Stones with your clients. Help them brainstorm various power words or positive messages of their own. Discuss ways they can use the stones, either for their own use or for giving them to others as a way to support loved ones and bridge positive connections to others.

- Have your client create her own set of stones that they can give to others.

Figure 3.1 Message Stones and Collaged Heart Stones

Materials:

- A collection of smooth stones.

- Acrylic paints.

- Paintbrushes, including one with a fine tip.

- Toothpicks (to add small details with paint).

- Varnish.

Directions:

1. Create a list of power words, mantras, and positive messages that you want to use in your collection. Refer to the list of words and phrases below for ideas if needed.

2. Rinse the stones and let them dry.

3. Paint one side of each stone one color.

4. Allow the paint to dry.

5. Use a paintbrush with a very fine tip to paint one word (or phrase) on each stone.

6. Allow the paint to dry.

7. Add patterns or designs around the word if there is room to do so.

8. Allow the paint to dry.

9. Use a paintbrush to apply a thin layer of varnish over the painted areas of the stone.

10. Allow the varnish to dry.

MESSAGE STONES WORDS AND PHRASES

- I can do this • Imagine • Speak up • Love • Silence
- Listen • Breathe • Peace • Give • Stand tall • Create
- Home • Calm • Freedom • Patience • Tranquility
- Bliss • Receive • Connect • Strength • Choice • Truth
- Laugh • Honesty • Courage • Express Yourself • Fly
- Reach • Honor • Nurture • Be kind • Rest • Appreciate
- Gratitude

COLLAGED HEART STONES

These cheerful stones are a delight to have in your office. They can be used for soothing—the client can look through the collection of hearts and see which ones appeal to them by color, pattern, or design. Heart Stones are also comforting "fidgets." You can leave them in a bowl on your desk and a client can hold onto one during a session. Alternatively, you can keep the stones in a jar for final sessions in which you are celebrating a client's successful completion of therapy. Allow the client to choose one of the stones to take with them to keep.

Regardless of how you use these stones, they are simple and inexpensive to make.

Materials:

- A collection of smooth, flat stones.

- Patterned papers—can be paper from scrapbook, newspaper, recycled papers, gift wrap, takeout menus, pages from a colorful book.

- Scissors.

- Decoupage glue.

- Small paintbrush.

Directions:

1. Cut hearts out of various papers. The hearts need to be small enough to fit on the stones.

2. Use your paintbrush to apply a thin layer of decoupage glue to the underside of a heart.

3. Apply the heart to one of the stones, and press down with the paintbrush to smooth out any air bubbles.

4. When the heart is completely flat against the stone, add a thin layer of decoupage glue over the heart.

5. Repeat for each stone.

6. Allow the stones to dry completely.

SQUEAKY WHEEL ADVENTURES

Squeaky Wheel Adventures (SWA) is a non-profit travel camp for children in foster care or other out-of-home care. SWA utilizes a custom, converted, vegetable-oil-powered bus to provide multi-day road trips which blend fun, adventure, self-exploration, environmental education, and stewardship.

Nature-based activities are the centerpiece of most SWA trips and include activities such as hiking, horseback riding, sea kayaking, camping, or just dangling our feet in a slow-running stream. Our small group size allows us to be flexible enough to take detours from our schedule. A stream discovered along the side of a hiking trail can consume an afternoon, a spontaneous wish to sleep under the stars can become a magical night, and an hour spent searching for four-leaf clovers can transfix a group of teenagers like a well-orchestrated activity never could. Return campers most often recount these types of events, which no one planned, no one paid for, and which unfolded spontaneously without any anticipation or expectation, as among their favorites.

The beauty of nature-based activities, oftentimes, is that each of us has the opportunity to create our own experience and to feel that moment fully in our minds and our bodies. Some endeavors challenge participants physically, others stretch them emotionally, and some simply allow for a moment of rest or careful observation. Afterward, each child has their own story to tell, shaped by a multitude of personal factors, which is different from anyone else's but which unites the group in a shared experience. What they take away might be mighty or small but, because it is shaped, felt and interpreted in their minds and in their bodies, it has the potential to leave a lasting impression.

Alyssa and Bryan Wolf
Squeaky Wheel Adventures
For more information, visit http://squeakywheeladventures.org/
about.php

Figure 3.2 The Squeaky Wheel Adventures bus

SQUARE FEET

Look around the grounds of where you work with your clients. For each participating client, mark an area that is about 12 in × 12 in (30 cm × 30 cm), a square foot—this can be marked with a flag, stones, string, or other boundary.

Go to the client's designated Square Foot every week or once a month with the client. Discuss and document what has changed or occurred since the last time you both visited. Try this ritual for several weeks (or even months) so the child can observe their area in different weather or seasons. Children can document if anything new showed up in their space, such as an acorn. They can note if anything is living there, such as grass or an anthill. They can measure how tall a plant is and then monitor if it grows even more. The longer the child observes what is going on in their Square Foot, the more changes they will observe.

Do not be surprised if your client becomes protective of the Square Foot after a while, or sad to end the ritual. The Square Foot activity helps to build connection between your client and nature because they start to understand just how much is happening in this teeny tiny area. Keep a journal or record of each visit because small details may seem insignificant. It can be easy for children to generalize and in the end say "not much happened in my Square Foot," but when you document all the details they'll have a reminder that a lot truly did happen—life, death, transformation, weather, seasons, and mystery all have potential to add to the story of the Square Foot.

The Square Foot also aids in mindfulness practice because a square foot space is quite small—your client will need to hone in on minute details in order to realize just how much life is happening or struggling in this small area.

Discussion and reflection:

1. What is your first impression of this space? Have you ever noticed this space before today?

2. Take a guess as to the stories this space might tell you if it had the ability to speak—do you think anything interesting or exciting has ever happened in this space before?

3. How is the Square Foot experience like getting to know people?

4. Now that you have visited your space several times, how do you think your Square Foot would describe you if it could speak? For example, would it describe you as gentle? Concerned? Curious? Uncaring? Bored? Is this similar or different than the way your friends or family might describe you?

5. Do you feel more connected and familiar to this space now than the first time you visited?

6. How does having familiarity with a space make you more connected to it? Would you have been angry if someone destroyed this Square Foot on day one? What about today? Why or why not?

EARTH LOOMS

Earth Looms are spaces between trees where kids can weave natural objects in and out of a premade "loom." The loom can be used for various clinical purposes, all of which allow for positive connection to others because the loom is a group effort.

Figure 3.3 An Earth Loom—this one was premade between two sticks and then tied to a tree

Clinical uses for earth looms

Grief work

Weave a nature-based item into the loom in memory of a loved one or event you are grieving. Items can also be tied onto the loom as long as they are lightweight. Flowers, leaves, grasses, and branches can be used metaphorically to represent the grief, a memory, or association with the person or event. For example, daisies could be woven into the loom in memory of a grandmother who loved daisies. A branch could be woven into the loom in memory of a sibling who passed away. The items remain in the loom and become part of a collaborative work of art representing and honoring the memories of loved ones and cherished moments.

Prayers, hopes, and positive messages

Children can write wishes, dreams, prayers, hopes and positive messages onto strips of muslin cloth and then tie the cloth onto a twig or stalk to weave into the loom. Use permanent markers to write the messages on the cloth strips. Clients can also draw a picture in place of writing.

This type of Earth Loom is a beautiful representation of the collaborative connection we all have to hopes and dreams. It gives children a place to communicate what they want for a better world and to see that other children like themselves have hopes and dreams like their own.

Rite of passage

You can also use an Earth Loom as a graduation ritual, a rite of passage, or a celebration for completing the program or therapy. When the client "graduates" they can choose a nature-based item to weave into the loom. In this regard, it represents their presence in the process of recovery, leaving a part of themselves behind (perhaps representing the challenges they worked on), as well as signaling hope to future clients that recovery and healing is possible.

Materials:

- Two thick branches or small tree trunks which are close together (it can even be a tree that has grown in a "V" shape).

- Yarn or twine.

- Nature-based materials such as feathers, grass, flowers, and sticks.

Directions:

1. Create horizontal rows of yarn: Tie several rows of yarn going from one tree trunk (or tree branch) to the other.

2. Create vertical rows of yarn: Tie yarn to the top row and when you get to the next row of yarn, loop the yarn around and continue to the next row. Continue this pattern until you

get to the bottom row of yarn and then tie it off. Repeat this step to create several vertical rows of yarn.

3. Clients can find nature-based items to weave into the loom.

4. Different clients continue to add to the loom over time.

DESTINATION ARTSWARM

Destination ArtSwarm is a migratory social arts program for kids in grades K-8 (ages 5–13). Over an eight-week period each summer we visit eight beautiful and inspiring places and then make art in and about the area. We use the natural materials we find on site and sometimes bring in other "ingredients" too. Using found materials in this way gives kids an intimate knowledge of a place.

Nature-based activities are an inherent part of this program. For example, one time the kids collected all of the materials they needed to build a beach fort from the beach itself. They found and used drift wood, sea debris, shells, seaweed, and broken bits of lobster traps and buoys. In addition to building the fort, we talked about the items we were finding, the industries the ocean affords us, and the storm that brought it all ashore, and so on.

The kids dig right into the project every time and work together to create a collaborative piece of art. Most of them don't think of themselves as artists but every one of them has a role, and in the end they've made something amazing together—in the case of the beach fort, something lasting! Friends visit the art and enjoy it and the kids feel part of something bigger and special.

I believe the program is beneficial to kids on so many levels. Getting them "unplugged," working with their hands, using their creative energy, socializing, building respect, building an understanding of nature, getting to know the environment, and feeling like a part of the bigger community are just some of the benefits of the program.

Pamela Tachibana
Destination ArtSwarm
For more information, visit www.facebook.com/ArtSwarm

Figure 3.4 Beach fort—a collaborative work by kids on the Destination ArtSwarm program, using found materials
Photo source: Tachibana

CREATING POSITIVE CONNECTIONS WITH ANIMALS AND PETS

Children have the potential to receive many benefits from having pets. These benefits include learning empathy, loving kindness, respect, nurturing, attachment, and positive connections. On the other hand, if children grow up in an environment where their pets or other animals are treated cruelly or neglected then the experience can have a *negative* effect on the wellbeing of the child and family.

I've worked in the mental health field for over two decades in several capacities. Like others working in this field, I know all too well that when animals are being abused it's a red flag that others in the home might be harmed as well. There are direct correlations between animal cruelty and domestic violence as noted by the American Society for the Prevention of Cruelty to Animals (ASPCA):

> In recent years, a strong connection has been documented linking animal abuse and domestic violence. A New Jersey study found that in 88 percent of families where there had been physical abuse of children, there were also records of animal abuse. In

Wisconsin, battered women revealed that in four out of five cases, abusive partners had also been violent toward pets or livestock. The National Coalition Against Domestic Violence conducted its own study in which 85.4 percent of women and 63.0 percent of children reported incidents of pet abuse after arriving at domestic violence shelters. The Chicago Police Department's Domestic Violence Program took a look at the criminal histories of animal fighting/animal abuse arrestees for 2000–2001 and found that approximately 30 percent had domestic violence charges on their records. There is legitimate evidence that the individuals involved in violent acts against animals present a danger to the public that must be addressed. (ASPCA 2013)

Therefore, it's important to address the wellbeing of the pets in the home because this ultimately has an impact on the wellbeing of the child as well.

In addition, many parents get pets for their kids in order to provide lessons in responsibility. However, many children are not ready to take on the responsibilities of having and keeping a pet, no matter how much they love the animal. They also may not understand the natural consequences of mistakes such as not taking the dog out on time, forgetting to feed the fish, leaving a door ajar, or leaving people food in an area where the pet can find it. Ultimately, it is the adult's job to care and provide for the pets even if the child has agreed to take full responsibility. Pets are not lessons—they are living beings who can feel emotions and suffer when not nurtured and cared for. When children have pets before they are ready to care for them, they can end up harming the animal or even killing them unintentionally. For children this can become a layer of guilt, shame, and self-hatred that only adds to the clinical issues you may be working on with them already. Therefore, if your client has a pet under the premise of "learning to be responsible," assess whether this is truly helping or potentially harming the child. If it has the potential to be harmful, have a discussion with the family about possibly reassigning responsibilities in order to assure that the pet is being cared for appropriately.

Also, if you are working with a family in which safety and/or substance abuse is an issue, make sure the family has a safety plan that includes the pets. Children are much less likely to worry about their pets when they know the family is aware of safety issues and has a plan to keep *all* family members safe, especially in emergencies.

Overall, children can be deeply affected by the way animals are treated in their homes. Based on the above concerns you can support the client in the following ways:

- During your assessments ask about the pets in the home.

- Create and provide a resource list for pet owners in your community that includes any or all of the following:

  ° food pantries that provide pet foods

  ° domestic violence shelters that partner with local police to assist victims of abuse

  ° pet insurance providers

  ° veterinarians who accept bartering as payment

  ° reliable pet sitters

  ° an emergency veterinarian contact person.

- If providing a resource list is too daunting (or there are too few resources to make a list), contact your local university or graduate school and let them know there is a need for this type of project to be compiled. The school may be able to set up an internship for a student in the social work field who could do this resource list and collaborate with local pet-friendly services.

- Assist the family with budgeting, if appropriate, to help them meet the medical and daily needs of the pets.

- Provide a safe place for children to express and process their feelings about their experiences with pets.

- Teach children skills in empathy and loving kindness so they can reap the benefits that pets have to offer, and vice versa.

Figure 3.5 Young children can learn empathy and loving kindness with animals—be a positive role-model for them
Photo source: Verow

One way that children learn empathy and loving kindness, besides experiencing it themselves, is through watching and learning from others. You can role-model this behavior when you are with clients. For example, if you work with young children, you can use puppets, stuffed animals, animal figurines, dollhouses, and barns as venues for role-playing nurturing interactions with animals. You can also bring in therapy animals if this is feasible and accessible to you. If you visit clients in their homes, show the animals in the home loving kindness as much as you can in a safe manner—this is role-modeling. If an animal is clearly sick or aggressive, you will want to keep your distance but you can certainly convey that the animal is worthy of love and respect through the way you communicate with and about the pet.

There are other ways to help clients learn loving kindness, connection, and empathy via caring for animals. You can include your clients in projects such as making and caring for bird feeders on the property where you work, putting out materials for the birds to make nests with, and encouraging clients to commit a random act of kindness toward an animal.

BIRD FEEDING

If you have the time and money to commit to feeding a few birds, then you may want to consider putting a birdfeeder on the grounds where you work. If you have a window in your workspace you could even install a small window feeder.

Many children love to nurture animals, if given the chance. Feeding birds is one way they can practice nurturing and kindness. If possible, make opportunities for clients to help care for the birds by filling a clean birdfeeder with fresh seed and hanging it back outside. Children who help you in this endeavor will start to feel ownership in helping the birds, which can bolster self-worth, encourage the child to continue nurturing behaviors, and provide a positive connection to the natural world.

If you work near a park where people feed the birds (e.g. pigeons or ducks) you could consider combining a walk with feeding these birds. Bring along a bag of organic (if possible) bread or crackers to feed to them.

You can also make your own treats for the birds with children who enjoy messy, sensory-rich activities.

BIRD TREATS

Materials:

- Pine cones.

- Nut or seed butter (peanut butter works great but if your client has a tree nut allergy you can use a seed butter, e.g. one made from sunflower seeds) or lard.

- Bird seed.

- String.

Directions:

1. Tie a piece of string to the pine cones so that you can hang them later.

2. Use your hands or a spoon to smear a layer of nut/seed butter or lard inside the layers of the pine cones.

3. Roll the pine cones in birdseed.

4. Tie the pine cones to tree branches.

Anytime you start feeding the birds anew, it can take some time for the birds to find your feeder or treats. Be patient and most likely they will come to visit!

NESTING SHOP

Another way you and your clients can help the birds is by making little nesting "shops." This is an activity that does not require much commitment or energy but it is still fun.

Purchase a suet feeder (not suet) for birds or use a small mesh bag for this project. (Some people like to reuse mesh-produce bags but if the fruit in the bag was sprayed with pesticides then this will not be good for the birds—if you use recycled materials, make sure they come from organic sources.)

Next, fill the feeder or mesh bag with scraps of string, ribbon, and even grasses. Make sure bits and pieces of the scrap material are poking out of the sides. Then hang the Nesting Shop outside. Birds will eventually come and take bits and pieces of these scraps home to add to their nests. If you or your clients are lucky, you may even spot one of the scrap materials in a nearby nest.

RANDOM ACTS OF KINDNESS TOWARD ANIMALS

Completing random acts of kindness toward animals can be helpful for children when 1) they want to commemorate and honor a pet, 2) they have harmed an animal and want to make amends, 3) they are feeling disconnected from the world or feeling depressed, 4) they have low self-worth or confidence, 5) they are working on relational skills such a nurturing, safe touch, respecting boundaries, and respect.

Here are various acts of kindness that can be considered:

- Turn in cans and bottles for money to donate to the local animal shelter.

- Make a poster about being kind to animals and hang it up (e.g. at the child's school, in the child's apartment building, at a public or community bulletin board).

- Speak up and speak out when others are being cruel to animals.

- Volunteer at the animal shelter (for older youth).

- Clean a pet's food and water bowl, and give them fresh food and water.

- Talk kindly to animals.

- Read a story to your pet.

- Donate clean towels, blankets, and stuffed animals to the local animal shelter.

Chapter 4

NATURE-BASED THERAPY AND GRIEF WORK WITH YOUTH BY KARLA HELBERT

Figure 4.1 Karla Helbert

Karla Helbert is a licensed professional counselor (LPC) with a therapy practice in Richmond, Virginia. Karla has worked as a therapist since 2000 and has experience as a psychotherapist, counselor, behavior therapist and group facilitator working with diverse populations of people of all ages, from many different walks of life. Her special focus areas are loss, grief and bereavement, anxiety management, Mindfulness-Based Cognitive Therapy, and working with people on the autism spectrum.

After her son died of a brain tumor in 2006, she gained a deep personal, as well as clinical, understanding of the difficult issues facing those grieving the deaths of loved ones. Karla, through her writing and therapy practice, helps people find their own pathways through the dark, but sometimes beautiful and always transformational, journey through grief.

Karla's first book reflects both her work in grief and bereavement as well as her speciality in working with those on the autism spectrum. *Finding Your Own Way to Grieve: A Creative Activity Workbook for Kids and Teens on the Autism Spectrum* was published by Jessica Kingsley Publishers in 2012.

I asked Karla to contribute her wisdom to this section of the book as she is well spoken and experienced in the topic of grief work. Following are some questions I asked Karla to address.

How do you incorporate nature-based activities into your work with young clients?

Depending on the setting and the child, we may simply take a walk around the neighborhood where my office building is located, or have a full session in the park or other natural location. When I worked as a counselor for a private school, we had a summer camp for five weeks as part of extended school year services. This was a great opportunity to work every day with kids in a natural setting—there were acres of woods, a lake, a garden, cabins, boats, and a swimming pool on the camp grounds.

It's easier to find interesting and engaging sensory activities outdoors where the ability to sense our connection with the earth is much more accessible. These activities include listening to as many nature sounds as possible with eyes closed or feeling the complete and total support of the earth while lying on the ground. I also use Mindfulness-Based Cognitive Therapy techniques and work with kids and teens on understanding they are not their thoughts—they can control the focus of their attention as well as their thoughts. Through this practice of observing, they begin to see they are connected to something greater than themselves. Nature intrinsically supports this truth. In grief work, or work with transitions (moving, changing schools, divorce), nature-based rituals are incredibly helpful. Nature is healing and supportive. Doing these kinds of rituals and other nature-based activities in a natural outdoor space, where all around growth and life is affirmed, allows kids to see and sense that growth and healing are naturally part of them as well. Nature adapts, adjusts, and accommodates all sorts of changes, and life always wins. Since we are part of nature, we can learn to do this too.

How do kids respond to the activities?

Kids almost always love nature-based activities because they understand intuitively the benefits of being in nature. All of us respond positively to being in fresh air, near green leaves, in the sun, feeling the breeze and being near other creatures who share our space on the planet. If we can be near water, a lake, stream, creek, river, or ocean, this can add another dimension to the therapeutic experience. We are part of the earth and kids know this is true, whether they are told or not. Nature-based activities allow the freedom to experience this in our bodies and minds.

Most often, kids are much calmer and grounded after nature-based activities. Kids who have difficulty opening up or engaging in therapeutic activities in an indoor space, very often will respond to the therapist outdoors. Simply walking side by side outdoors while talking can mitigate the discomfort some kids may feel in an indoors therapy office. While a therapist may not feel that his or her office is an uncomfortable place (and actually, most therapy offices are comfortable and welcoming places), a child may perceive sitting in a static space as difficult. They may have difficulty with eye contact or maintaining the traditional "talk therapy" model. Outdoors, they feel more relaxed, less of a patient, more of a person. Additionally, many children are able to engage much more readily when moving their bodies and when they are able to direct excess energy elsewhere.

What benefits, if any, do you see of kids interacting with nature in this way?

Opportunities and encouragement for children and teens to be outdoors are much more limited than in years and decades past. For kids who live in a city, the location limits their opportunities, but even kids who live near woods and other abundant natural settings often do not go outdoors as often. Simply enjoying the benefits of nature and being familiar with the natural world can reduce stress, increase feelings of wellbeing, and help to decrease anxiety and depression.

In therapy work, I see bringing kids and teens (as well as adults) into a relationship with nature as a literal and symbolic way of helping them understand that they are connected to something larger than themselves. This concept is easily illustrated by discussing the planet as a whole, and ourselves as part of the ecosystem and humans as one of the many species on the planet. Often we discuss mythological perspectives of Gaia and the earth as a living organism in her own right who supports us totally and how we are connected to her and part of her. We are all the children of Earth. These notions can be instinctively supportive when a child or teen feels alone or distressed. The hope that once therapy is done, one day the child or teen may go outside on their own and allow their stress and sadness to melt into the earth, or that they may perform their own journeying ritual when they need guidance informs much of my nature-based work with kids. Nature can always be a place that they can turn to when they need support and connection.

Can you share a few nature-based activities that you use with your clients?
Yes. Any of these can be used as exploratory, expressive, or meditative practices for individuals or for groups. They may also be altered slightly to make them very appropriate for use as grief or transition rituals.

WATER PAINTING

Materials:

- Access to any natural body of water.

- Water-safe shoes.

- Heavyweight watercolor paper.

- Watercolor paints (individual paint palettes usually work best as they can be transported easily).

- Cup for extra water.

- Paintbrushes.

This activity can be done individually or with a group. Group members may be invited to share their experiences if they wish after the activity is completed.

Find a natural body of water. This can be a creek, pond, stream, river, lake, or the ocean. You may wish to try the exercise with different bodies of water and see how your feelings may be different, images may be different, and how your paintings turn out differently.

Wearing water-safe shoes, or going barefoot if safety issues have been resolved (no danger of broken glass or other obstacles that could create injury to bare feet), wade into the water carrying your paper. If your body of water is deep, wade out only to your knees or just above the knees.

First, simply walk around in the water.

Now begin to notice things: Notice how the water feels against your skin. Notice the temperature of the water and the feel of the air against your skin. Notice how your skin reacts. Do you have goose pimples? Is the water warm, cool, or cold? Notice how the temperature of the water may change depending on where you are standing or if you are moving. Notice how the water feels as it moves against your skin. Which direction is its current? Are you walking or standing against the current, or walking with it as it flows?

> Make sure you feel steady and balanced. When you feel balanced, gently shift your weight to one foot. Lift the other foot up and notice how the air feels against your wet skin. How is it different from how your dry skin feels? Notice how the water runs down your leg, your foot. Slowly lower your foot, then find your balance on two feet again. Shift your weight to the other leg and lift your opposite foot from the water. Does your balance feel different on this side?
>
> How does the bottom of the body of water feel? Squishy, rocky, sandy? Can you feel it between your toes?
>
> Notice how the light plays on the surface of the water. Notice reflections of the environment on its surface. What can you see reflected? Sky, trees, sunlight, your own body?
>
> What sounds can you notice? Are there sounds of nature, birds, or insects? Can you hear sounds of humans in the distance or nearby? Notice the sound of the water. Is it still and calm, making little sound at all? Does it lap against the shore or crash? Does it trickle or flow? What are the water sounds you hear?

When you are fully present with the water, imagine that the water is communicating with you. Perhaps the animals and plants that live in the water are also communicating with you. What would the water and the creatures who call it home say to you? You can close your eyes if you like or leave them open. If your eyes remain open, allow your gaze to be soft, looking at nothing in particular. Allow the message of the water to come. It may come in words, phrases, music, pictures, images. Continue to allow the water to speak to you until you feel that it has sent the message it had especially meant for you. Do not worry that it's just you making it all up. Just listen and see what comes.

When you feel ready, take your watercolor paper and submerge it in the water. Swish it around a bit. After a short time (remembering that you don't want to leave the paper in for too long), remove it from the water. Say goodbye to the water for now and walk back to the dry land.

Use your watercolors to paint your experience in and with the water. If you like, you can paint a portrait of the water itself, or yourself as the water. You can paint the message the water sent, or whatever other wisdom you received from the water, as it communicated to you.

When your painting is done, stretch it out so that it will dry flat. Feel free to keep it for yourself or share it with others. You can also write in your journal about your experience with the water.

For a grief ritual

Before submerging the watercolor paper:

Stop for a moment, simply standing still in the water as it moves around your feet, ankles, and legs. Allow yourself to acknowledge the hurt you feel due to the absence of the one you love. Notice where you are feeling the hurt—in your body, your heart, your belly, your chest? If you want or need to cry, you have permission to cry. You are safe here. Imagine your tears can merge with the water and flow toward the ocean. If you are in the ocean, imagine your tears, salty like the sea, merging and mixing with all the water covering the planet. Imagine that you don't have to carry all of the pain right now. Imagine some of the pain being carried away on the current or tide of the water. In a lake or a pond, imagine the pain dissolving and dispersing, the body of water taking it in, diluting and removing some of the pain from your body and spirit.

When you feel ready, submerge your watercolor paper and continue with the rest of the activity as specified above.

SHADOW DRAWING

Materials:

- A tree large enough to sit near or under and whose trunk is large enough to support your back.

- A sunny day to allow for shadows to be cast.

- Drawing paper of your choice.

- Drawing implement of your choice.

- Other medium for color (optional).

This activity can be done individually or with a group. Group members may be invited to share their experiences, if they wish, after the activity is completed.

On a sunny day, find a tree that seems to invite you to sit beneath it. Take a seat on the earth with your back to the trunk. For a moment, sit quietly. Close your eyes if you are comfortable doing so. If not, allow your gaze to be soft and fuzzy, focused on nothing in particular. Begin to notice your breath moving in and out of your body. You don't have to do anything to change it. Simply notice. Allow your belly to fill a little more deeply with air and then your chest, shifting to deep breathing for a few breaths. When you feel calm and centered, allow your breath to return to normal.

As you inhale, imagine your body absorbing the energy of the tree. Notice how the energy of the tree feels. Each tree is unique, just like each person. The energy you notice from the tree may feel calming and soothing, supportive and nurturing, or strong and protective. Your tree will send you the energy that it has to give. As you exhale, allow your stress, sadness, disappointment, fear or other bad feelings to sink into the tree. Allow the tree to take it from you. Imagine the tree absorbing the bad feelings, sending them down through its trunk, out to its roots and deep into the earth. Imagine the tree filling your body and spirit with its particular energy—loving, healing, supportive, energizing, calming—whatever the tree has to give, it will give to you.

Place your hands on the trunk of the tree and send a message of thanks for its support and love. It is also okay (and recommended!) to hug the tree if you wish.

You can do that part anytime you wish, on a sunny day or cloudy day, a rainy day or even at night time.

Continue on for the shadow drawing:

When you feel ready, find a spot under the tree where you would like to sit to do your drawing. Find a place where the sun shines through the branches of the tree, allowing shadows of the leaves and branches to be cast onto your drawing surface.

Pick up your drawing implement and begin to trace the outline of the shadows cast by the tree on your paper. You can stay in one area of the paper, or you can move your lines all over the paper, or draw in one continuous line. Draw how it feels right to you. The breeze may also be blowing and the shadows may not remain still—this is okay.

Continue in this way, shading if you feel like it, or drawing only with lines. When you feel you are finished, stop, thank the tree and the sun for their help, and move to a different spot.

In a different place, or later on, look at your line drawing of the shadows. You can decide that you are finished with your drawing or you can continue by adding color and connecting more lines or adding to the piece. Notice whether you see any shapes or figures emerging in the drawing. You can use color to fill in spaces where your lines crossed each other. You can add other elements or fill in spaces where you think maybe a flower or a face might go, perhaps an eye here, a table leg there, an elephant trunk over there, a spiral or a circle. Connect lines and create a heart—do whatever you wish. The piece is yours.

For a grief ritual

Imagine that your loved one can communicate with you through the spirit of the tree. Don't worry that it's imaginary. It can be as real to you as it needs to be. Imagination doesn't mean unreal.

When you see the shadows move, imagine that these are picture images sent to you from your loved one. Imagine that the two of you can create this piece of art together.

When you take the picture away to study it in a different place, you can continue to imagine that your loved one is sending you a message through the picture. What images, shapes, letters or words might emerge from the shadow lines?

You can save the picture and hang or store it in your room or in another safe place where you can look at it anytime you like to remind you that your loved one is with you all the time. You can also write about it in your journal or share it with others.

TREE MEDITATION

Materials:

- A forest, small or large, or a wooded area with plenty of trees to choose from.

Facing the trees, have a seat on the earth. If you are working in a group, form a circle if you like.

After getting comfortable, allow your body to begin to come into the present moment. Close your eyes if you feel comfortable, or if not, allow your gaze to be soft and not focused on any particular thing. Begin to notice the way the earth feels beneath your body. Notice where your body is touching the ground (your bottom, legs, ankles, feet, your back or head—if you are lying down) and where it is not (the small spaces behind your ankles, just behind your knees, your arms, your face). Become aware of the temperature of the air, how your skin feels where it is covered with clothing and where it is exposed to the open air and the breeze. What sensations can you notice throughout your body? Notice if you feel jumpy or itchy, calm or heavy. You don't have to change it, or do anything about it, just notice.

Notice what you can hear. In all directions, to your right, left, behind and in front of you. What sounds of nature can you notice? What human sounds do you notice?

Breathing in through your nose, what smells can you notice? Grass, pine, your own scent? How many different smells can you notice? You may only notice the freshness of the air, or something completely different.

Moving your attention inward, with the secure knowledge that you are supported entirely by the earth, begin to notice your thoughts. Notice what thoughts are moving through your mind. Let your thoughts come in and go out, like clouds floating across a summer sky.

Bring your attention and thoughts to a problem you may have been worried about. Think of how things are going for you in your life right now and form a clear thought about the thing in your life that you are most worried about. What do you need the most help with right now? Know that it is okay to think of these things because you are safe and secure.

When you are ready, open your eyes and let your gaze wander over the many trees in the forest until you see a tree that reminds you of yourself. When you are ready, go to that tree. Sit at the base of the tree, stand next to the tree, put your arms around the tree—do whatever feels right to you. Communicate your worries and fears to the tree, let the tree absorb your concerns. Tell the tree what you have been going through. Know that the tree hears and takes in your hurts. When you are ready to leave the tree, thank the tree for taking some of your worries from you.

Return to your space. You can share what the experience was like with the group or with your therapist. You may also write in your journal or create another kind of art about your experience with the tree.

For a grief ritual

After the grounding, allow your thoughts to turn to your grief. Let your mind be aware of your loved one whom you love and miss greatly. Know that it is okay to feel sadness that this person has died. Know that it is natural to feel grief. Know that you are safe to have these feelings and that you are not alone.

Choose a tree that reminds you of yourself, or of your grief. Go to that tree. If you wish, you can place your hands on the tree, or put your arms around the tree. Try to imagine comforting the tree as if it were a friend of yours who is going through hurt or pain. Tell the tree why it reminds you of yourself. You can speak out loud or you can simply think these thoughts. Imagine the tree can hear you. Imagine that the tree wants to help you. Imagine gathering up some of the hurt you are feeling into the palms of your hands and putting your palms on the tree's trunk. Give some of the hurt you are feeling right now to the tree. Thank the tree for supporting and helping you.

Return to your space. You can share what the experience was like with the group or with your therapist. You may also write in your journal or create another kind of art about your experience with the tree.

JOURNEY TO THE CENTER OF THE EARTH

Taken from Native American traditions of power or spirit animals, this activity is a visualization which helps a child or teen connect with a member of the animal kingdom as well as to be in touch with difficult or complex feelings and potentially gain insight into their own experiences in life. The animal can be seen or presented as a guide, a protector, or a source of comfort. If the child or teen wishes, the image of the animal may be called up in future times of stress to serve as a focal point for attention or meditation. During the visualization, the therapist or group leader can drum softly and rhythmically if drums are being used. Remind the group or individuals to stay within the sound of the therapist's or group leader's voice.

At any time, it is extremely important for the therapist or counselor to process information received through this exercise with the child or teen and to support them throughout the process to ensure that they feel entirely safe throughout.

Materials:

- An open natural space, wooded or not (although a forest or wooded area may provide a more interesting experience and more exploration of the space and feelings).

- Blanket, towel, or cushion for sitting or lying on (optional).

- Drum(s) (optional).

- Journal or art supplies for drawing or writing after the visualization (optional).

- A small stone or flower (optional).

You are invited to wander and explore the space until you find a place you feel drawn toward. Once you get to this place, look for a crevice, a hole, a hollow space in a tree, or any other kind of space where you might imagine a small creature could enter and travel down into the Earth.

Once you find your space, have a seat on the ground near that space where you can see it clearly. If you have a blanket, towel, or cushion, feel free to sit or lie down on that if you like. You may close your eyes, or focus your gaze softly on the opening you have located. If your eyes are closed, continue to see the entry space in your mind's eye. Mentally picture yourself growing small enough to fit easily into the space. Remember throughout your journey, that you are absolutely safe, protected, and secure. The space you have located and entered is not a scary or threatening space.

Once you enter the space and move a bit further inward, you might imagine a staircase or a pathway opening up before you. You are invited to follow the path that has opened just for you, noticing that it slopes gently downward. Moving further and further down into the Earth, notice whether the setting around you changes. Are there lights illuminating your way? What do they look like? How does your environment appear as you continue to journey downward into the Earth? This is your own creation and experience; your path can look however you choose.

You might imagine coming to a space where your path or walkway opens or widens into someplace else. Perhaps you may experience your space as a large underground cavern, wide and spacious. Or, perhaps your space remains small, fitting just perfectly around your body, helping you to feel secure and held. Everyone's experience is different.

Once you feel that your downward journey to the center of the Earth has reached its deepest point, visualize or imagine a doorway or another kind of opening onto a completely new scene or landscape. Step through that new opening.

What do you see now? Notice how your landscape appears. Is it an underground room or the top of a mountain? A sandy beach or an open prairie? Is it a wooded glen or a desert plain? Notice the details. Is it day or night, morning, afternoon or evening? What season is it? Can you see the sun or is there cloud cover? What are the features of your landscape? Is there plant life? What is the terrain?

Once you become familiar with your landscape, allow the image of an animal, a bird, a reptile, or an insect, to enter into your landscape. When your animal arrives, ask it to share with you its special attributes or qualities. Ask it to give you assistance in this difficult time of your life. Ask it a question about how to manage something difficult that you are worried about or struggling with. Commune with your animal in whatever way feels right to you. If the animal appears in any way hostile, be assured of your safety and know that perhaps now is not the time to communicate with your animal. When you are ready, thank the animal and return to the surface of the Earth and to the present moment.

You can leave your small stone or flower as an offering of thanks to your animal and to the Earth in exchange for the help that you received. If you do not leave an offering, simply place your palms on the Earth and imagine sending your thanks into the Earth as a vibration of positive energy into the ground. If you like, share your experience with others. Journal or create art about your experience. Draw a picture of your animal or write down the messages you may have received from your animal.

For a grief ritual

The visualization can be presented in the same way as above, but with a focus on the child or teen receiving comfort, support, or wisdom from the animal guide specific to their loss and/or their individual grief journey. Some grieving individuals may visualize or imagine the animal as bringing messages from their deceased loved one. This is okay.

If you would like more information about Karla's work, you can visit her website at www.karlahelbert.com.

Chapter 5

GARDENING FOR WELLBEING

Gardening is a multi-beneficial activity for wellbeing because it combines fresh air, exposure to the natural environment, exercise, sensory input, Vitamin D, and relaxation. As mentioned in the Introduction, it can also aid in the production of serotonin due to exposure to microbes in the soil. A garden can also be a form of art, creative expression, and a place for play and exploration.

If you decide to embark on a gardening adventure, there are several types of gardens to choose from including flowers, vegetables, rocks, and water. There are also many themes to choose from. If you plan to plant any of the gardens in this chapter, you may need to do additional research (i.e. online or via gardening books) to make sure you live in the right climate for the plants.

OUTDOOR THEMED GARDENS

GIANT GARDENS

Plain and simple, "giants" are a larger-than-normal variety of plant such as giant sunflowers, giant pumpkins, giant corn, giant onions, and so on. Plants that are considered "giant plants" need plenty of deep, rich soil to grow in, and plenty of room to spread out. But if you have the gardening space to grow these behemoths, kids can find it fun to watch them grow. Plant pole beans and add a wooden garden stake with a castle painted on it for a "Jack in the Beanstalk"-themed garden.

TEENY TINY GARDENS

Just like Giant Gardens are full of giant plants, Teeny Tiny Gardens are full of miniature plants. These plants can be grown in containers, as the plants do not take up much room. Mini varieties of vegetables can be a delight for children to grow because they are perfectly sized for small hands and snacking. The small plants are also perfectly sized for snacks at tea parties and picnics with stuffed animals, dolls, and friends.

Some vegetables that come in mini versions are tomatoes (such as cherry tomatoes and yellow pear tomatoes), cucumbers, peppers, baby potatoes, mini pumpkins, baby melons, miniature sized okra, and petits pois (petite peas).

CURIO CABINET GARDEN

Fill this garden bed with plants that arouse the curiosity of your child and allow them to experiment and be creative with the things they grow.

- Giant walking stick cabbage: You need a warm climate to grow these because they can take up to 300 days to grow. But the cabbage grows on a long stalk that can actually be used as a walking stick after harvesting.

- Snake gourds: Snake gourds grow in the shape of snakes. They are long, slender, and curvy gourds. After harvesting they can be cured and then painted with snake patterns and snake faces.

- Money plant: After the flowers bloom on this plant, translucent, silver seed pods will follow. Kids can use the pods for pretend coins.

- Cucumber in a bottle: Grow a regular cucumber plant. When the cucumbers first start to emerge, place the opening of a bottle over the cucumber. Check on the cucumber a few times a week. As the cucumber grows bigger, push the cucumber deeper in the bottle as needed. Eventually the cucumber grows full size in the bottle. You can cut the cucumber off the vine and voilà—the child has a cucumber in the bottle. They can amaze their friends and see if anyone can figure out how he got it in there.

- Graffiti pumpkins: If you are growing regular-sized pumpkins, try this fun trick. When the pumpkins are small (about the size of an adult fist) you can carve a design, name, quote, or picture into the flesh of the pumpkin. Use a toothpick, wooden skewer, or ballpoint pen to draw or write with. Only carve through the top layer of flesh so as not to damage the pumpkin. As the pumpkin continues growing it will scar in the places where you carved. The words or pictures you created will grow with the pumpkin.

- Spaghetti squash: The flesh inside the spaghetti squash is stringy like spaghetti and is a wonderful substitute for actual pasta if you need a low-carb or gluten-free replacement. There are many delicious options for eating this squash and kids will find it amusing to see how squash could have any resemblance to spaghetti.

MEDICINAL GARDEN

Teens and young adults may appreciate creating a garden based on medicinal plants. You can buy books about medicinal gardens or research "medicinal plants" online. Extra research is needed with medicinal gardening to make sure you use the correct part of the plant once harvested. Some plants will be grown for their leaves and others for their roots. However, if you have a budding healer in your midst, then this garden is a unique opportunity to learn about the healing power of plants. There are multiple medicinal plants all over the globe, but here are a few examples:

- *Echinacea*—used for immune support.
- *Chamomile*—used for its calming properties.
- *Peppermint*—used to settle tummy troubles.
- *Elderberries*—used for immune support.
- *Lavender*—used for its calming properties.
- *Arnica*—used for physical and emotional trauma, bruising and sprains.
- *Aloe vera*—a succulent used for treating burns.
- *Feverfew*—an anti-inflammatory.

SALSA GARDEN

Devote a vegetable bed entirely to salsa. Plant a mix of the following vegetables and herbs for the zestiest salsa ingredients. If you do not already have a favorite salsa recipe, ask your friends or research a recipe to fit your taste buds. Some people prefer scallions over onions, some want both. Some people detest the flavor of cilantro and others love it. Find the right salsa ingredients for you and your family and then enjoy planting the perfect flavor combination of salsa plants.

- Tomatoes.
- Tomatillos.
- Onions.
- Garlic.
- Scallions (spring onions).
- Green pepper.
- Hot peppers.
- Cilantro (coriander).

PIZZA GARDEN

Just like the Salsa Garden, the Pizza Garden is filled with plants to give your homemade fresh pizzas extra-fresh ingredients and flavor. What does your family like on their pizzas? Try planting an entire garden devoted to this favorite meal of so many children.

- Tomatoes.
- Green peppers.
- Broccoli.
- Onions.
- Basil.
- Oregano.

KIDS' CORNER

Kids' Corner in Bar Harbor, Maine has been providing high-quality child care and early education on the coast of Maine since 1990. With over 40 children enrolled on a daily basis we have a dedicated team of teachers who recognize that each child has unique talents, learning styles, and personalities.

We believe the most important work of children under the age of six is to develop self-confidence, a positive self-concept, empathy, and to experience successful conflict resolution.

Part of the dynamic curriculum we provide to support these skills involves planting and caring for a 25 ft x 25 ft (8 m x 8 m) organic garden. The children learn the intrinsic value of a small seed and, every step of the way, they come to realize the importance of caring for their garden. In turn, the care they have placed on watching their garden grow from seed is the same care they are taking of their body as they nourish it with fresh vegetables that they themselves have grown.

We also learn to care for other living things through visiting farms, aquariums, natural history museums, and taking nature walks. What better way to plant the seed of awareness and caring at a young age? How we approach these aspects of life lay the foundation for caring as we age.

We are a community-based child care center encouraging the children to learn by doing. Not a day goes by that the children don't go home dirty and in need of a good bath. To us, this is a sign of a successful day in the life of a preschooler.

Lori Krupke
Kids' Corner, Inc. of Bar Harbor, Maine
http://kidscornerbarharbor.com

Figure 5.1 The children at Kids' Corner learn how to grow an organic garden
Photo source: Krupke

COLOR-THEMED GARDENS

Children tend to have at least one favorite color. A color-themed garden can be a wonderful way to celebrate your child's passion for their favorite hue. I have listed plants to consider for each general color, but keep in mind that some plants show their brightest colors underground where you won't see them until harvest time. For example, if your child wants an orange-themed garden and wants to grow carrots, make sure you explain that the orange part is in the ground and won't be visible until you pull the carrots up. You will only see the bushy green carrot tops. If the child wants vegetables or fruit that are visibly orange on the exterior, then make sure you plan your garden accordingly.

Also, many flowers come in several different or mixed colors. If you want specific colors of a flower you can sometimes special order or buy just one color. *Cosmos*, for example, commonly come in mixed colors of whites and pinks. However, you can also buy singular colors of *Cosmos*. Do some research and see if your favorite flowers can be bought in one color.

- Reds:
  - Vegetables and fruit—tomatoes, sweet red peppers, hot red peppers, red cabbage, strawberries, raspberries.
  - Flowers—geraniums, tulips, *Salvia coccinea*, nasturtiums, scarlet bee balm.
  - Plants with red roots—radishes, beets, red potatoes.
- Oranges:
  - Vegetables and fruit—orange tomatoes, cantaloupe, butternut squash, orange peppers, pumpkins.
  - Flowers—marigolds, orange daisies, zinnias, poppies, orange nasturtiums.
  - Orange roots—carrots, sweet potatoes.
- Yellows:
  - Vegetables and fruit—yellow pear tomatoes, yellow summer squash, yellow wax beans, spaghetti squash, rutabagas (swedes).
  - Flowers—sunflowers, *Coreopsis*, yellow lilies, yellow lupine, yellow foxglove, yellow marigolds.
  - Yellow roots—golden beets, yellow onions, "Yukon Gold" potatoes.

- Greens:
  - ° Vegetables and fruit—lettuce, spinach, Swiss chard, green beans, beets and carrots (only the green parts show in the garden), tomatillos, okra, celery, honeydew melon, peas, cucumbers, zucchini (courgettes), watercress, cabbage, Brussels sprouts, endive, Chinese cabbage.
  - ° Flowers and plants—green gladioli, *Hosta*, *Astelia* "Silver Mound," lamb's ears.

- Blues:
  - ° Vegetables and fruit—blueberries.
  - ° Flowers—delphiniums, forget-me-nots, blue pansies.
  - ° Blue roots—blue baby potatoes.

- Purples:
  - ° Vegetables and fruit—eggplant (aubergine), purple endive, purple cabbage, purple lettuce.
  - ° Flowers—lupines, pansies, lavender.
  - ° Purple roots—purple carrots, purple-topped turnips.

- Whites:
  - ° Vegetables and fruit—cauliflower.
  - ° Flowers—white *Cosmos*, daisies, *Alyssum*, petunias, white foxgloves.
  - ° White roots—parsnip, garlic, white potatoes, parsnips, shallots, jícama (Mexican yam).

- Pinks:
  - ° Vegetables and fruit—pink is a tricky color for fruits and vegetables (e.g. although watermelon is green on the outside, the flesh is pink and sweet on the inside).
  - ° Flowers—*Cosmos*, lilies, pink daisies, petunias, pink delphiniums, pink foxgloves, pink geraniums.

GARDEN RAINBOW

To create a rainbow garden you will need to research which flowers grow in your region of the world.

1. Choose a variety of flowers that fit your climate in the following colors: red, orange, yellow, green, blue, and purple. Be mindful that not all flowers bloom at the same time. The easiest way to plant a rainbow is to go to a local gardening center and actually buy the flowers that are currently in bloom in the colors you need. You can choose a green herb in place of flowers since most places will not have flowering green plants.

2. Prepare the garden space for your flowers. If your garden is square or rectangular shaped, you can choose to either do your rainbow colors in stripes to fit the space, or you can draw a bowed rainbow in the soil and plant your colors along the arced rows.

3. Plant and care for your plants according to the directions that came with them.

BUTTERFLY GARDEN

The first themed garden I planted with my son was a Butterfly Garden and it was well worth it. Not all the plants grew as we expected, and none of them looked as gorgeous and lush as they looked on the seed packets or catalogue, but we did get some beautiful flowers and plenty of butterflies for our efforts! Over the years we have become better gardeners, but I still look back at that summer and cherish the memory of planting that first garden together.

You will need to plan your garden according to where you live and what butterflies are native to your area. Do your research and plant the flowers that will attract native butterflies to your area. In addition, butterflies need two different types of plants for their survival. "Nectar plants" are the plants and flowers that butterflies will feed from. "Host" plants are plants they will lay eggs on and/or eat as caterpillars. Butterfly gardening takes a little planning but it's worth it. It's wonderful to look out at a garden and see all the butterflies feeding. It's also exciting to discover a chrysalis among the flowers.

As much as possible, eliminate the use of pesticides. Help your butterflies thrive by keeping a toxin-free yard.

BOOK-THEMED GARDEN

Does your child have a favorite book? Or do you? A garden based on a favorite book is a creative challenge—the opportunity offers an innovative way to combine a passion for reading with an interest in gardening.

Gather details from your child's favorite book, such as where the story takes place, any foods or plants that are mentioned, and landscape cues. Based on all of these clues, plan a garden around the book. For example, if you were going to plan a garden around *Alice in Wonderland* by Lewis Carroll, you might consider the following:

- "Dark-eye" *fuchsia* and columbine—these flowers show up in many illustrated versions of the book.

- Pansies—some varieties of pansies have a "face" in them which mirrors the fantasy-like talking plants and creatures in *Alice in Wonderland*.

- Roses—the Queen of Hearts has a rose garden.

- Ferns—ferns also show up in many illustrated versions of *Alice in Wonderland*.

You could also add embellishments to your garden that are not plants at all, but enhance the connection between the garden and the book theme. Examples of such embellishments could be faux red mushrooms with white spots, a tea cup left behind in the garden (perhaps with a hens and chicks plant growing inside it), plant markers made from playing cards, a pink flamingo or croquet ball, or a bottle and key hanging from a fencepost.

Brainstorm ideas for a garden based on a cherished book and see what creative ideas you can come up with!

BOOK-THEMED GARDENS FOR CHILDREN OF ALL AGES

Megan Emery is a Teen Librarian at a public library. She has an abundance of creativity and a passion for children's literature, which made her a perfect candidate in helping me with this section of the book. I asked Megan to "design" three gardens based on popular children's books which could inspire others who want to create gardens based on literature.

Preschool: *The Lorax* and *Horton Hears a Who* by Dr. Seuss

- Purpose: Play and movement are the main focus of this colorful garden. In the center is a spiral-floored play space surrounded by a graduated retaining wall. On the other side of the retaining wall are hidden nooks among trees reminiscent of truffula trees and striped grasses. The nooks provide secret and safe spots where children can whisper to one another using whisper tubes. Sensory play is encouraged in a cascading water feature built into the rising retaining wall complete with lemon-, mint, and chocolate-scented plants bordering a thin, babbling brook that winds around the exterior of the spiral center.

- Plants: Zebra grass (*Miscanthus sinensis*), Scotch pine (*Pinus sylvestris*) topiaries in multiple shapes, silk trees (*Albizia julibrissin*), *Allium* "Gladiator," African lily (*Agapanthus*), blue-flowered garlic (*Allium caeruleum*), *Allium* "Hair," "Hakuro-nishiki" dappled willow (*Salix integra*), creeping phlox (*Phlox subulata*) in multiple colors, lemon thyme (*Thymux x citriodorus*), chocolate mint (*Mentha x piperita*), English daisies (*Bellis perennis*), iris "Kentucky Bluegrass" (*Poa pratensis*), lamb's ear (*Stachys byzantina*).

- Hardscape: Whisper tubes in multiple colors, stone patio with a spiral of flagstone paving surrounded by light-colored gravel, gradual and cascading water feature, flagstone retaining wall that spirals around the entire garden, building the garden bed from ground level to 3 ft (1 m) high.

Middle school: *Charlie and the Chocolate Factory* by Roald Dahl

- Purpose: Willy Wonka's own incredible, edible garden is recreated in this space that is filled with color, candy-like scents, and textures that are irresistible to the touch. A rainbow of plants which attract hummingbirds and butterflies encourage nature to surround garden visitors. Fruit trees and edible flowers are mixed into each garden and all plants are labeled to explain what's edible and what's not.

- Plants: Chocolate mint (*Mentha x piperita*), lemon thyme (*Thymux x citriodorus*), spearmint (*Mentha spicata*), English thyme (*Thymus vulgaris*), bee balm (*Monarda didyma*) in multiple colors, bleeding heart (*Dicentra spectabilis*), butterfly bush (*Buddleia davidii*), chocolate daisies (*Berlandiera lyrata*), chocolate cosmos (*Cosmos astrosanguineus*), "Black Magic" elephant ear (*Colocasia esculenta*), "Blue Moon" wisteria (*Wisteria macrostachya* "Blue Moon"), heliotrope (*Heliotropium arborescens*), lamb's ear (*Stachys byzantina*), nasturtiums, "Strawberry Candy" daylilies, "Blue Dragon" daylily, strawberries, "Red Haven" peach tree, "Rainier" cherry tree, "Honeycrisp" apple tree, "Red Gold" nectarine tree.

- Hardscape: Tea cups on stakes for planters. Ornate Victorian-style outdoor benches and table sets in rainbow colors, cocoa bean shell mulch.

Tween/Teen: *Harry Potter* (HP) series by J.K. Rowling

- Purpose: This space combines the whimsy of a wizard's world with a sense of play in comforting, intimate sitting areas—beautiful to look at and supportive of introspection and relaxation. Multiple sitting areas under a variety of climbing plants on a large exterior pergola are offset by classic English-style gardens—wild looking combinations of flowers and vegetables reminiscent of the books. The highlight is the flying car from the second book, renovated to last outdoors and tucked into a tangle of climbing plants for a private sitting space to relax in.

- Plants: Sensitive plants (*Mimosa pudica*), mandrake (*Mandragora*), weeping willow (*Salix babylonica*), mammoth pumpkins (*Cucurbita maxima*), "Lumina" pumpkins (*Cucurbita maxima* "Lumina"), lamb's ear (*Stachys byzantina*), bee balm (*Monarda didyma*) in multiple colors, "Blue Moon" wisteria (*Wisteria macrostachya* "Blue Moon"), "Golden Tiara" clematis (*Clematis tangutica*), "Fourth of July" climbing rose, *Coreopsis*, bearded iris "Pink Attraction," *Gerbera* in multiple colors, red cabbage roses.

- Hardscape: 1966 Ford Anglia. Long, narrow wooden tables with Victorian cloches and tabletop greenhouses for mandrakes and sensitive plants. Fairy lights (strung above table area reminiscent of candles in the Great Hall). Tree cross-section table and stumps for seats (concrete cast if necessary). Plant markers with botanical information, historical info regarding magical background other than HP series and literary factoids from the HP books. Large, dark wood pergola surrounds the exterior.

"FIVE SENSES" GARDEN

A garden for the five senses is a true delight for children. Kids can interact with these plants to touch, hear, taste, smell, and see a variety of sensory-rich plants.

Plants for the five senses:

1. Touch: Irish moss, lamb's ear, gold thistle, strawflowers, hedge woundwort, Jerusalem sage, pussy willows, gayfeather, mimosa, hens and chicks, and trees (for touching bark).

2. Hear: Rattlesnake grass, quaking grass, love-in-a-mist, wind chimes, and water features for added sound.

3. Taste: Berries, fruits, vegetables, edible flowers and herbs. You can also grow herbs and other plants that can be used in tea and have a "tea tasting" section of your garden.

4. Smell: Herbs not already in the "Taste" section of the garden, lavender, honeysuckle, snapdragons, fragrant lilies, lilacs, sweet peas, roses.

5. See: Chinese lanterns, red hot pokers, Sculpted boxwoods, garden sculptures, "whirligigs," and pinwheels that add movement to the garden. You can also add a small reflection pool (e.g. a birdbath) to the garden.

Directions:

1. Create a plan or blueprint for your garden before planting. Keep in mind you can also make this garden using five containers if necessary. You can label garden sections or containers with "Taste me," "Listen—hear me," "See me," "Touch me," and "Smell me" for clarity.

2. Divide a garden space into five areas based on your garden plan or blueprint. You may have one garden section larger than another—it's likely the areas will all be different sizes.

3. Put your plants in the ground according to their growing and planting directions.

4. Label the areas of the garden so that people know which section belongs to which sense—you do not want them tasting all of your plants! Section off or mark the areas clearly.

FAIRY AND GNOME GARDENS

Fairy houses, fairy villages, and gnome gardens are enchanting mini landscapes that appeal to kids and adults alike. You will need to consider a few options when planning your fairy or gnome garden, such as size, matching plants to your climate, and available natural materials.

Figure 5.2 Scene from a Fairy Garden

Fairy gardens can be any size. Many people grow fairy gardens in containers because fairies and gnomes are small creatures so they don't need very big landscapes. Container gardens are appealing because they do not require a lot of care or room. But the garden size is your choice. If you have more room to spare and you are passionate about a fairy- or gnome-themed garden, then you may want to use a larger space. Some people even clear an area in their yard or woods to allow kids (and adults) to come and build fairy houses in their "community."

Search the internet or gardening books to find which miniature variety or naturally small plants will grow in your area. If you live in a shady woodland area, your choices for plants will be very different than another who lives in the desert. Some naturally small plants include hens and chicks, creeping thyme, and moss. You can also buy miniature varieties of many plants such as mini *Hosta*. There are online resources specifically for planting fairy and miniature gardens and you can get a lot of information about tiny plants for your climate at these sites.

Here are some useful tips in planning and planting your Fairy Gardens:

1. Create a groundcover: Moss, creeping thyme, baby tears, blue star creeper, and wooly thyme will cover an area of the garden where you would like to create a lawn, forest floor, or hillside effect in your landscape. If you live in a hot climate where groundcovers won't grow, you can use varying patterns of crushed stones to create changes in landscape.

2. Add "trees" and "bushes": Rosemary, hens and chicks, and *Sedum* can be used for pretend trees and bushes in your Fairy Gardens. For drier climates you can use succulents and even pine cones to mimic trees. Adding these "trees" creates dimension and detail to make the garden space look more like a true landscape.

3. Create pathways: Add tiny pathways through your Fairy and Gnome Gardens with flat stones or sticks. You can lay them down on top of the groundcover or establish the pathways first and add groundcover around it.

4. Add faux mushrooms: You can purchase garden picks that look like miniature mushrooms. Red topped mushrooms with white spots look especially fairy- and gnome-like.

5. Add miniature objects to fit the landscape: Before you purchase any miniature garden accessories, try to repurpose what you already have. Kids often have teeny tiny toys that belong to dollhouses, building sets, and play sets that are

not being used. I have saved time and money by repurposing play items this way. You can also look for these pieces at yard sales and second-hand shops to save money.

FAIRY HOUSES AND GNOME HOMES

If you are new to Fairy Houses and Gnome Homes, do a search on the internet to view the amazing level of creativity that goes into building these magical houses and gardens.

Some homes are elaborately built, but the amount of detail you add to them is completely up to you. Some of my favorite Fairy Houses have been the ones that children made with a few sticks, grass, or rocks.

Figure 5.3 A simple Fairy House made from sticks and bark

Fairy Houses and Gnome Homes are not required to be permanent structures. Nor are they required to be part of a garden. Some people like to build them when they visit natural spaces such as beaches, hiking trails, or under and around trees. Other people create permanent Fairy Gardens in which they incorporate the Fairy Houses and Gnome Homes as part of the landscape.

Here are some Fairy House and Gnome Home ideas for beginners:

- Buy or repurpose a birdhouse and turn it into a Fairy House. You can paint it with a fairy theme or you can glue acorn caps or other natural items to the roof tops and house siding to make it look appealing to fairies and gnomes.

- Use broken, clay plant pots as fairy houses by turning them on their side or upside down. Sometimes the broken area of the pot can act as a doorway into the house.

- Create a mound of dirt and plant a groundcover over and around the mound. Place a miniature fairy or gnome door at the base of the mound to look like a little home is inside the hill. The door can be made from scrap wood or you can buy "fairy doors" and "gnome doors" online from specialty shops.

- Turn a tree stump into a fairy living space. The flat area or top of the tree stump can have a mini living space at the top. It could be a reading nook, a hideout, a mini play area, a picnic spot, a bathing area, or other space where a fairy or gnome would want to come and visit.

- Use larger rocks as house walls, then cover the top of the rock house with a large piece of bark. Make sure to only use found bark that is already off the tree. Do not remove bark from a tree as it can damage the tree.

- Use several sticks of similar size to create a teepee-like house. You can use string, garden twine, or ribbon to tie a knot around the top of a bundle of sticks. Place the stick bundle vertically on the ground (ribbon side facing up) and spread the sticks out along the bottom. Maneuver the sticks until they are stable and can stand on their own.

- Lean sticks against a tree, stump, or rock to create a fairy or gnome shelter.

Once you have created the main structure, add embellishments. Houses can be decorated with flowers, grasses, shells, acorn caps, and so on. Look around for natural materials that can be added to your house.

FAIRY HOUSE ACCESSORIES AND EXTRAS

Fairy House "Accessories and Extras" include everything from lawn furniture, picnic tables, sign posts, and gazing balls that can be made from natural materials and added to the fairy house or surrounding area.

Gather various sticks, twigs, acorns, shells, and other nature-based items. Play around with the materials to see what can be glued together to create different features for the house. For example, sticks can be glued together to make benches, tables, and chairs. Shells can be transformed into pools, bath tubs, and birdbaths. Acorn caps and pine cone seeds can be glued onto rooftops for shingles. Experiment with your materials to see what you can create, but here are a few quick and easy accessories.

Lamp post

Materials:

- Small but sturdy stick.

- Acorn with the cap attached.

- Yellow paint.

- Paintbrushes.

- Varnish.

- Glue—industrial-strength glue works best for durability and weather resistance but it is not kid-friendly, so if the kids are doing the gluing, then use regular white glue.

Directions:

1. Use the stick as the lamp post.

2. Paint an acorn (but not the cap) yellow and let it dry.

3. Apply a thin layer of varnish to the acorn cap and acorn and allow it to dry. You may need to apply the varnish to one side

of the acorn and let it dry. Then flip it over and apply it to the other side and let it dry—acorns tend to roll all over the place, which makes crafting with them a bit tricky.

4. Glue the acorn to the top of the stick. The cap will look like the lid of a lantern and the yellow acorn will look like a lit lantern.

5. Push the lamp post into the dirt where you need it.

Sign post

Materials:

- Wood chip or small stick shaped like a rectangle (for the sign).
- Small but sturdy stick (for the post).
- Acrylic paint.
- Paintbrush.
- Glue.

Directions:

1. Paint a word or symbol onto the wood chip or small stick you are using for the sign. (The sign can be for a location, a shop, a direction, or a traffic sign.)

2. Allow the paint to dry.

3. Glue the sign onto the post and allow the glue to dry.

4. Insert the sign post in the dirt where you need it.

Gazing or crystal ball

Gazing balls are used as a garden accessory—you can make this mini version for your fairy garden.

Materials:

- Industrial-strength glue.
- Wide, round, branchy stick that can hold the marble (you can also use a golf tee).

- Clear or shiny marble.

Directions:

1. Dab a little glue to the stick or golf tee where the marble will sit.

2. Place the marble on the glue and hold it there until the glue sets enough to hold it; or set the gazing ball in a spot that it will stay balanced while the glue dries.

3. When the glue has dried completely, set the gazing ball in the center of a mini Fairy Garden.

ROCK GARDENS

Rock Gardens are fabulous when you want to design a space that needs almost zero maintenance and is free of many allergens. They are also versatile for any climate. The downside of Rock Gardens, however, is cost. Rocks are expensive and delivering them costs money too. But if you are planning a Rock Garden here are some creative ways to incorporate kid-friendly spaces where kids will want to play:

- Boulders provide climbing and jumping opportunities for kids.

- Smooth boulders are blank canvases for chalk—let your kids draw and write all over the rocks.

- Boulders can be used for many different purposes. For example, as seats for reading or journaling, seats for meditation or quiet reflection, as a dining table for picnics, as a pretend fire truck or other large vehicle, as a pirate ship or other imaginative play prop, for hiding (as in hide and seek), and so on. If you have a child and even one large rock, you can count on the rock getting a lot of play.

- Incorporate a gravel, crushed stone, or paving stone walkway in your garden for added kid appeal. Many kids love pathways.

- If you use flat paving stones or bricks in any of your garden space, allow kids to color and draw on them with colored chalks.

ROCK ART IN YOUR GARDEN

Gather a variety of rocks and make pictures with them in the empty spaces of your garden, or place them around strategically to make patterns in the soil. You can make swirls, spirals, heart shapes, and many other designs to add to the beauty of your garden.

Figure 5.4 Rocks used to create a spiral (placed on the top of a tree stump near a garden space)

Figure 5.5 Rocks used to create a picture of flowers on the soil

MINI SCULPTURE GARDENS

Sculpture Gardens are outdoor spaces where sculptures are featured as the main attraction. Flowers and foliage plants are often part of these gardens too, but the main focus is the outdoor art that shares the same space. Children are natural curators when it comes to Sculpture Gardens. Kids love pinwheels, "whirligigs," painted garden stones, garden statues, benches, wind chimes, garden art made from found objects, bottle trees, and sculpted plants and trees.

COMMUNITY GARDENS

Some communities, rural and urban, have gardens where community members can rent a plot of space to grow their own plants. If you do not have a yard, patio, or other space for gardening, then community gardening can be a wonderful way to get your hands in the dirt and grow your own food. Use your favorite search engine to look up "Community garden," followed by the area in which you live.

INDOOR GARDENS

TERRARIUMS

Terrariums are plants grown inside a glass or plastic container. Plants that need a lot of moisture can be grown in a *covered* terrarium. High-moisture plants include moss and ferns.

Materials:

- Glass or plastic container (e.g. fish bowl or fish tank, wide and shallow glass vase, or glass jar).

- Pea gravel or small pebbles to fill the bottom of your container.

- Sphagnum moss.

- Organic soil.

- Plants that will fit in the container.

- Jug of water.

- Little plastic figurines.

Directions:

1. Wash and dry your terrarium container thoroughly.

2. Place a 1–2 in (2.5–5 cm) layer of pea gravel or pebbles onto the bottom of the container. This will act as a drainage layer for your plant roots.

3. Put a thin layer of sphagnum moss on top of the gravel. This layer will help to hold the soil in place. Without a layer of sphagnum moss the soil will settle down into the pebbles and you won't have adequate drainage for your plants anymore.

4. Add a thin layer of soil into the terrarium.

5. Place your terrarium plants on top of the soil and space them as needed.

6. Add soil all around the plants until the roots are completely covered. Add a little more soil to make sure the plant is stable and will stand on its own. Pack the soil in around the plant if necessary.

7. Give your plants a little drink of water.

8. Add figurines in and around the plants. Many kids love this part of creating terrariums. If your child has animal or people figurines (or other plastic and glass knick-knacks), they can add them to their terrarium.

SUCCULENT-THEMED GARDENS

Succulents are fascinating plants. Many times they grow with intriguing lumps and bumps, patterns, and spikes that add visual detail to their appearance. Kids can create a mini Succulent Garden and then add plastic figurines to make a desert-themed landscape.

The directions for a succulent garden are the same for making terrariums, except you can plant your succulents in any container. I have planted succulent gardens in vintage enamelware pots and children's tin cups as well as planters bought from a garden shop. Whatever container you choose, fill the bottom of the container with pea gravel or pebbles, cover with sphagnum moss, and then add a little soil. Place your succulents in the dirt and cover the plant's roots. Add more soil as needed to make sure the plants are stable.

Add fun, desert-themed figurines to your succulent garden, such as pretend tumbleweeds, horses, cowboys, skeletons or skulls (you may have some mini ones from Halloween or other spooky event).

Make sure to water your succulents according to the directions on the plant label. If you are ever unsure of how often to water your plants, you can look in a plant book or find the information online.

DOMED PLANT WORLDS

Domed Plant Worlds are specific terrariums that you can buy in a kit or even create on your own. They are round and dome-shaped to allow for maximum humidity. The plants are arranged in themed collections and have added figurines to complete the "world." The plants in these collections tend to be more expensive, harder to find, and higher maintenance. For this reason, they are better for older kids and adults to plant and manage. You will also need to use an online search engine to track down the most suitable plant seller for your country. Some countries do not allow plants to be mailed overseas. You can buy the domes and other shaped terrarium containers from online retailers as well.

Here are some themes and plant ideas for Domed Plant Worlds:

- Mars attack: Plants that look out-of-this-world and alien-like include the peek-a-boo plant (also known as the eyeball plant), many succulents, Venus fly traps, small pitcher plants, and any bioluminescent mushrooms. You can also add tiny alien figurines or a crashed UFO to your dome to add an even more dramatic feel.

- Gnome dome: The dome can be filled with a variety of mosses and ivies. Tuck a little gnome figurine in the foliage.

- Carnivorous plants: Venus fly traps, pitcher plants, and sundews are all carnivorous plants—they have differing ways to capture and digest insects. You could add insect figurines or objects with a science fiction theme to the dome.

WINDOWSILL GARDEN

Windowsill Gardens are exactly what they sound like—miniature gardens that fit on a windowsill. Many people grow herbs on their windowsills but you can grow flowers and even some vegetables, too. You can purchase a planter that fits on your windowsill (either several small pots or one long narrow trough-shaped container) or you can recycle and reuse containers you already have.

Windowsill friendly-plants include herbs, leafy green vegetables, and small varieties of flowers.

Directions:

1. Choose a windowsill that gets plenty of sunlight. South-facing windows get the most sun exposure.

2. Fill the bottom layer of the planter or container with pebbles to help with drainage.

3. Fill the planter with garden or potting soil about three-quarters full.

4. Plant your seeds to the depth indicated on the seed packet.

5. Make sure to pay attention to the watering needs of your plants. Do not over-water your plants but do make sure you water regularly.

MINI LAWN FOR YOUR FEET

For those of us who live in cooler climates, a mini green lawn in the dead of winter is just dreamy. And it's easy, too! Buy a plastic tub, fill it with soil, and then sprinkle grass seed on it. Keep the grass seeds moist until they germinate, and put your mini lawn where it can get sun exposure. For example, you could put your mini lawn in a sunbeam each day, moving it as necessary to get exposure. Or, if you have a naturally sunny area of the house, leave the tub in that space. Eventually your grass will grow and you will have a little lawn to put your bare feet on!

WHIMSICAL CONTAINER GARDENS

Whimsical Container Gardens combine recycling and a sense of humor. They can be grown in almost any container that has a space for soil and a plant including boots and shoes, wagons, baskets, luggage, a saxophone, or a tire.

Directions:

1. Always wash and dry the container before you begin the project.

2. Add a layer of pea gravel or small stones to the bottom of the container.

3. Add a thin layer of sphagnum moss.

4. Add soil to the container.

5. Add your plants.

Figure 5.6 Various containers re-purposed for Whimsical Container Gardens

Part II

NATURE IS FUN

Does this sound familiar—"I'm bored" or "There's nothing to do outside"? It can be a challenge at times to get kids outdoors to play. For some it even seems impossible—between lack of outdoor play spaces, concerns about safety and supervision, or convenience (let's face it, sometimes it's so much easier to give in and let the kids play a video game so you can get some work done)—there are obstacles to getting our children outside and connected to the natural world. However, it is not impossible.

In this section of the book I provide ideas that encourage kids to interact with their natural environment using play, imagination, self-expression, and creativity.

SAFETY FIRST

- Make sure there is adequate and appropriate supervision for children at all times.

- If going on trails or to unfamiliar places, bring a First Aid kit and cell phone in case you get lost or someone gets hurt.

- Use the "Buddy System" when exploring new places. Make sure each person has someone to stick with.

- Keep track of your surroundings.

- Stay hydrated.

- "Carry in, carry out"—this means whatever you bring with you, leaves with you. Do not litter.

- Apply appropriate insect repellent and sunscreen as needed or required.

- If there are trails, follow the rules of the trail. Rules of the trail are often posted near parking areas and trailheads.

- Make sure you know your environment well enough to explore it safely. For example, poison ivy can look different depending on the location and season so it is best to avoid all plants with clumps of three leaves. Teach children, "Leaves of three, let them be." Be mindful of any other poisonous or dangerous plants and animals in your area when exploring near trees and forests.

- Always wear protective clothing, such as shoes, when exploring natural areas.

- When leaving grassy or wooded areas it is best to do a quick check of your clothing and skin for insects. Ticks are common hitchhikers, for example, so make sure you do not have any ticks or insects on you or the kids before you leave.

Chapter 6

GENERAL OUTDOOR ACTIVITIES

SCAVENGER HUNTS

Scavenger hunts are an activity where children try to find items on a list. If a group of children are having a scavenger hunt, they might try to see who can find the items first, or look collaboratively as a group. Create a list of items for your child to find outdoors. If you are heading to a park, the beach, a playground, and so on then create a list based on objects likely to be found in that area.

Items that might go on a scavenger hunt list:

- Something round.

- A twig in the shape of a Y.

- Something that starts with the letter _____.

- A bottle cap.

- An acorn.

- A leaf.

- Two different colored pebbles.

- Something green.

- Something scratchy.

- Something that made you smile.

NATURE JOURNALS AND SKETCHBOOKS

Create or buy your child a sketchbook that is filled with blank pages. Bring it with you in the car, on walks, on trips, to the park, and so on, and encourage your child to stop and observe different places. Allow them to take a few moments to draw or write about what they see. When my son was three we started a nature journal and sketchbook for him. We kept a bag with his sketchbook and some pencils in it and took it everywhere for a few summers. Once he got used to the process, he started to ask to stop at places to sketch. At times he wanted to sketch a bridge or a pond. Sometimes he would ask to make a special trip somewhere just so he could sketch there, such as a monastery or a lighthouse. By age four he added an extra sketchbook to his bag, which he called the "guest sketchbook." If we were visiting with family or friends he would ask them to sketch with him in the guest sketchbook.

Years later I came across these books and was amazed at how such a simple tradition made an impact on him. His drawings are simple and mostly unrecognizable at his young age but I love to look at the pictures and remember him sitting by a riverbank, or next to a clump of flowers, or even sharing a porch swing with a loved one while they both sketched. The process helped him to slow down and just observe with his senses and capture the moment without technology but with creative expression.

Here are other ways to use a nature journal or sketchbook:

- Use words, sketches, doodles, or other art form to document what lives and grows in your neighborhood. What kind of trees/animals/flowers/birds?

- Visit a spot each week and document what is happening there or what changes occurred in the past week. Are there any new plants growing there? Are leaves changing size or color? Are things healthy and thriving, or in ill-health or dying? Are there any new signs of visitors here, such as animal prints in the mud or droppings left behind?

- Draw or illustrate a visual checklist of animals, plants, or other life forms that are in your area and that you would like to see. When you find them, check them off or put a sticker next to them. You can even do a little research to find out if there are rare or endangered species in your area and add them to your checklist for a challenge.

Figure 6.1 Find a place outdoors to draw or write about your natural surroundings

PLEIN AIR ART

Plein Air Art is an art form that translates as "art in the open air." When you see artists on the side of a river, on the beach, or in the park painting at their easels—that's an example of Plein Air Art.

Many kids enjoy creating art in the outdoors, too. Put a bag together with various art supplies, such as paints, colored pencils, bottled water, paintbrushes, a clipboard (use a clipboard in place of an easel), and paper. Then head to a natural space to let your child create their own art in the "open air." Sunsets, clouds, bodies of water, fields, and trees are great subjects for children to paint and draw outdoors.

Figure 6.2 Plein Air Art—painting the lighthouse with watercolors

MINIATURE OUTSIDE WORLDS

A child can combine their existing toys and figurines with the natural world to curate these miniature landscapes used for imaginative play. If you do not have a yard to play in, go to a local park or public space instead.

Following are just a few examples of miniature worlds—see what other worlds your child can come up with.

Dinosaur world

Find a spot outdoors that is rich with foliage, tall grasses, and plants with big leafy stalks where your child can play with their dinosaur figures. If the dinosaurs need a pond or lake, bring a small pan to fill with water (bring bottled water and fill the pan when you get to your destination). Your child can even dig out an area for the pan to sit in so that the pan is hidden in the dirt. Rocks can be used as mountains or turned into landslides and meteors.

Fairy tales

Figurines of kings and queens, dragons and unicorns, wicked witches and fairy godmothers can go outside with your child to play.

Create dragon lairs, dungeons, and wishing wells by digging holes in the dirt.

Make secret gardens or masquerade areas near flower beds or garden spaces.

If you are at the beach, build sand castles for all the characters.

Figure 6.3 Seashells and a figurine are used as props in fairy tale play

Horse ranch

Bring a toy barn or stable outdoors for your child's horse figurines or other farm animals. Create a pond by filling a pan with water. Then divide the land into areas to make different fields—a work field, a grazing field, and a riding field. Your child can set up their horses and animals in different areas of the ranch.

Figure 6.4 Horse figurines being played with outside

Car garage

Use sticks and bark to build a temporary garage for toy cars. Do not take bark directly off of trees however—look for sheets of bark that have fallen from a tree. If you live near a rocky area you can also use the rocks as part of your garage in place of bark or sticks. Either way, build a temporary structure for your child to bring their cars to for repair.

Figure 6.5 Cars line up for repair work

BACKYARD PLAY KITCHENS

Children can pretend to have a kitchen in the backyard, where they make and bake mud pies, grass stew, and sand cakes. Set aside any old pots and pans, recycled containers, and utensils that can get dirty and messy. Set them outside in a special area for kids to play with.

Kids will naturally designate areas for a stove, sink, and so on—let them use their imagination and figure out ways to use the natural landscape as a kitchen.

PICNICS

Many children love the novelty of eating outdoors. Try experimenting with picnic spots and picnic foods to get your child and family out of doors and seeing new places. For example, try a fall picnic in the park when the leaves are changing colors—bring apples, dried fruits, or trail mix to snack on. Go to a desert area and have a desert-themed picnic with pita bread, hummus, and dates. Attend a "Shakespeare In The Park" event and have a picnic on a blanket while you watch the performance. You can also have picnics at drive-in movies, during a sunrise or sunset, in the rain, on a mountain, at the beach, on a rooftop, and so on. The opportunities are limitless, so brainstorm a picnic you and your kids might enjoy.

Figure 6.6 Having a picnic at the beach

One of my favorite types of picnics is a winter picnic. Many people associate picnics with warm summer days. However, winter offers a unique opportunity to enjoy eating al fresco in a whole other environment. Here are some winter picnic ideas:

- If you have a thermos or two, fill up a thermos with hot chocolate or other hot beverage. You can also fill a thermos with hot soup, macaroni and cheese, or other warm comfort food. I love the feeling of being outdoors in the cold and having something warm to eat or drink.

- Pack a wool blanket or something you can sit on in the snow.

- Try a winter picnic at night. When there is snow on the ground, a night picnic is magical—bring candles or lanterns to put in the snow and enjoy a late night picnic under the stars.

PARKS, TRAILS, AND PUBLIC SPACES

Many countries and states offer parks, trails, and historical sites that are open to the public—some even free of charge. These are wonderful places to explore, play, and learn.

LETTERBOXING

Letterboxing is an activity done around the world where you follow clues to find "letterboxes" that are hidden near trails, parks, and historical sites. Letterboxes are typically plastic boxes that hold a book, a rubber stamp, and an ink pad. As a participant *you* also have your own book, stamp, and ink pad. Stamps are significant in letterboxing as it is a mark of your identity as well as an art form highly respected in this activity. Participants can go online to a letterboxing website to look for clues to locations of letterboxes. Then it is up to you to go and follow the clues, and sometimes solve riddles, in order to find the letterbox. When you find the letterbox, you leave your stamp in the book to mark that you have found it. You also mark your own book with the stamp that is in the letterbox as a confirmation that you found the letterbox at that location. To go letterboxing you will need the following:

- A blank book.

- A rubber or foam stamp.

- An ink pad.

- Access to the internet.

Go to the letterboxing website at http://letterboxing.org to look at geographical locations. Although letterboxing is more common in North America, there are listings at this website around the globe. Letterboxing is an activity that is fun for all ages because it involves problem solving, puzzles, looking for clues, getting outdoors in natural spaces, exploring, collecting stamps from all the letterboxes you visit, as well as all the adventure that comes with seeing new places.

Letterboxing was the "go to" activity for my son when he had friends over to play when he was younger. We would look up local places that had hidden letterboxes, pick up his friend(s) and then go on a letterboxing adventure. These trips were often combined with picnics—always a plus. From lighthouses, mountain tops, farms, a monastery, and several state parks we visited many places as we collected our letterboxing stamps. If you are heading out on a long road trip, it is also a bonus to look for letterboxing locations along the way. This works especially well for children who need to get out and stretch their legs on road trips.

Figure 6.7 Finding a letterbox on a mountain trail

GEOCACHING

Geocaching is similar to Letterboxing but instead of following written clues you follow navigational directions in the form of global positioning system (GPS) coordinates. You need a GPS or Smartphone to go Geocaching. When you get to your coordinates, you try to find a Geocache, which is a hidden container. The container will contain a log book and sometimes even a "treasure," which would be a small trinket or item. If you take the treasure item, you must leave something of equal value for the next person to find. There are Geocaching websites that provide information and membership to play, such as www.geocaching.com.

CAMPING

Camping can be a fun adventure for children. If you do not own your own camping equipment you may be able to borrow some from a friend or try "car camping." Car camping means you simply sleep in your car instead of a tent or camper.

For first-time campers it is usually recommended to go to a campground where amenities and supplies are accessible, and activities are provided for kids. Many campgrounds also offer swimming pools and playgrounds.

I started taking my son camping when he was three. We have always kept things simple when it comes to camping because we only go a couple of times a year. We have a tent, two sleeping bags, two foam pads and a cooler.

Figure 6.8 Tent camping next to a brook

When we are heading out on a camping adventure we bring money for firewood (many places ask you not to bring your own because you could carry in harmful or invasive species in the firewood) and money for food. We stop at the natural food store on our way and fill up the cooler with a few meals, water, juice, and snacks. Hot dogs and sausage (yes even the vegetarian ones) are an easy camping food since you can put them on a stick and cook them over a fire without needing grills, pots, or pans. We typically camp for a night or two and sometimes go out to eat if it is rainy. Camping can be as lax and low key as you want it to be. Some people even camp on their rooftops in cities, in their backyards in suburban areas, and even their living rooms indoors.

For the adventurous campers, however, the sky is the limit. If camping is the type of outdoor activity that you and your children enjoy, you can explore places further away from home and for extended periods of time. Many campgrounds are even starting to offer unique camping experiences on their properties—K.O.A. camping in the USA, for example, has started to offer streamliners that people can rent and other fun alternatives. This summer my son and I are camping in a caboose on a K.O.A. property.

NATIONAL AND STATE PARKS

National and State Parks can offer the best of what nature has to offer in your geographical area. You typically need to pay a fee to enter these parks but the cost is well worth it. Some parks will even offer a day when the fee is waived, so if you are on a budget, search online to see what National and State Parks are near you and whether they have any "free pass" days. This way you can plan ahead and save some money.

Parks offer a variety of activity including hiking and walking trails, swimming areas, wildlife habitats, and more. One of my friends and her husband have taken their children to several National and State Parks and I am always amazed at the sights they see and the experiences they have. The following are some of my favorite photos from their adventures.

Figure 6.9 Crawling up the sand dunes
Photo source: Guertin

Figure 6.10 Descending the sand dunes
Photo source: Guertin

Figure 6.11 Descending the ladder
Photo source: Guertin

Figure 6.12 The family posing as Joshua trees
Photo source: Guertin

Figure 6.13 On the Bear's Hump
Photo source: Guertin

PUBLIC TRAILS AND HISTORICAL PLACES

On a smaller level, towns, parks, conservation trusts, and privately owned spaces sometimes offer access to trails and historical places for little to no cost. Some of my favorite places to enjoy the outdoors with my son have been in such areas. Search online or call your local town office to see if any such areas are accessible near you. Forts, lighthouses, historical homes, gardens, and monasteries are some of the places you might be able to visit for free or little charge.

Figure 6.14 On a historic tour
Photo source: Guertin

FARM VISITS

Farms are a wonderful place to bring children because they get a first-hand look at where and how food is grown and raised. Some farms offer more hands-on activity than others but the following are examples of some of the wonderful opportunities that visiting a farm might offer:

- Pick-your-own options: Pick your own fruit, flowers, and vegetables such as apples, pumpkins, corn, or sunflowers.

- Hayrides, wagon rides, horse-drawn carriage rides, tractor rides, sleigh rides.

- Petting "zoo," where kids can interact with the animals.

- Corn mazes, where farmers create a maze in their corn fields for people to navigate through.

- Season-related projects, such as visiting a maple sugar house, making apple cider, or having a community picnic to celebrate the harvest.

- Letterboxes: As mentioned in the section on Letterboxing, we have visited a couple of farms that had letterboxes which added to the fun of visiting a farm. If your favorite local farm does not offer a letterbox, you can ask them to add one.

Figure 6.15 Farms are wonderful places to see where food comes from
and visit the animals
Photo source: Krupke

NIGHT TIME PLAY AND OBSERVATION

Night time offers opportunities for nature-based play and adventure that cannot be done during the daylight hours. Even kids who are afraid of the dark will find some of these activities irresistible.

People often forget just how many amazing events happen at night. Meteor showers, "Northern Lights," lunar eclipses, fireflies, and other natural phenomena are wonderful to observe and experience at all ages, but especially for children. These events are truly magical.

SHADOW PUPPETS

Large tree trunks and boulders provide a natural backdrop for creating shadows. Try one of the following shadow puppet activities outdoors.

Hand shadows

Hands can be formed into various positions to create shadow puppets that look like birds, coyotes, alligators, and more. If your child is naturally inquisitive and patient, then you can challenge them to create their own. However, if your child needs added inspiration and instruction, you can use your local library or the internet to find books and instructions on making specific Hand Shadows.

Figure 6.16 Making Hand Shadows outdoors

Leaf shadow puppets

Find large leaves and then use a stick or sharp rock to tear and poke holes to make faces in them. Hold the Leaf Shadow Puppet by the stem and shine a flashlight in front of the leaf so that it casts a shadow on the tree trunk or rock.

Figure 6.17 Shadow Puppets made from leaves—the stories the kids told with these puppets were completely entertaining

TIN CAN LANTERNS

Tin can lanterns are a joy at night time and many kids love the feel of carrying their own lantern and walking with them. We made these lanterns one night for a special occasion—a meteor shower. The kids made lanterns at sunset and later on we all walked to an open space in the dark, the kids leading the way with their lanterns. We watched the meteors and then walked back home. The kids had so much fun with their lanterns that we used them again and again for night walks for the remainder of the summer.

Materials:

- Recycled tin cans (labels removed, washed and dried).

- Water and a freezer.

- Hammer.

- Nails.

- An eye hook screw (one per lantern).

- A long sturdy stick.

- Wire.

- Small candle (if young children are doing this activity you may want to opt for a battery-operated tealight candle).

Directions:

1. Fill your tin cans ⅔ full with water and put them in the freezer. Let them freeze overnight.

2. Once the water is frozen, use a hammer to punch nails through the tin in random order or in a pattern. The ice makes the can solid so that the tin doesn't collapse under the pressure of the hammered nails.

3. Make sure there are plenty of holes for the light to shine through your lantern.

4. Make two holes near the top of the can. The holes need to be opposite each other. These will be the holes where the wire will go through to hold the lantern.

5. Place the lantern in warm water for several minutes. The ice will slide out more easily this way. If you are not in a hurry, you can leave your lantern in a sink or outdoors to let the ice melt on its own.

6. Attach an eye hook screw to your stick. Toward the top of the stick is best. If you have trouble getting the eye hook in

the wood, you can use a thumbtack or pushpin to get a hole started.

7. Slide a piece of wire through the hole of the eye hook.

8. Bring one end of the wire through one of the top holes on your lantern.

9. Bring the other end of the wire through the other top hole.

10. Check the length of the wire—you will want to make sure the lantern hangs far enough away from the stick so that the candlelight is not near the stick—at least 6 in (15 cm).

11. When the length is adjusted, trim any excess wire and then twist the wire into place.

12. Place a candle in the tin can. If using a wax candle, you can melt some wax to the bottom of the can to help secure the candle in place.

13. Wait until the child is holding the stick and then light the candle in their lantern.

14. Remind the child to keep their hand steady and not swing the lantern. The lantern will swing naturally as the child walks but too much motion will cause their candlelight to go out. Bring extra matches or a lighter with you in case this happens.

15. Keep children with lanterns under adult supervision at all times.

METEOR SHOWERS

Meteor showers are events where meteors can be observed in the night sky more often than other nights. You can search online to get the dates and locations for meteor showers near you. Here are some tips for watching meteor events:

- Mosquitoes and other biting flies love night time, so cover up or use bug spray to keep the flies from biting.

- Get away from light pollution so you can see the meteors better. You may need or want to drive to a darker location.

- Try to find an open space for viewing, such as a field or a beach. However, we have watched many meteor showers from the front lawn with success.

- Lawn chairs that recline back, towels, blankets, and foam pads can be used to lie on. Your neck will thank you if you find a spot to lie down rather than leaning your head backwards.

- Allow a few minutes for your eyes to adjust to the dark and the night sky.

AURORAL DISPLAYS

If you live in the Northern hemisphere you might know these as Northern Lights or Aurora Borealis. If you live in the Southern hemisphere you might know them as Southern Lights or Aurora Australis.

Auroral displays are caused by collisions of charged particles in the atmosphere near the Earth's poles. During an auroral display the sky becomes distorted with waves of different colored lights. The lights can change and shift color. These events often increase and intensify after solar flares and solar storms. Reds, greens, pinks, and blues can be seen in the night sky. If you live closer to one of the Earth's poles (as opposed to closer to the equator) then you have a much higher chance of viewing an auroral display. For your best chance, run a search online to see if any auroral events are happening near your area anytime soon. You can also sign up for alerts via email from websites or even download an app on your phone if you have one. You will also want to get away from light pollution for your best chances of seeing auroral displays.

LUNAR ECLIPSES

Lunar eclipses happen when the Earth is blocking light from the sun from reaching the moon. Two lunar eclipses happen per year, sometimes more. You can search online to find out when lunar eclipses are happening in your area. A total lunar eclipse is beautiful to watch because the moon will look red or have a reddish tinge to it.

Lunar eclipses are also a fun excuse to eat moon pies with your kids. A moon pie is made of two round graham cracker cookies that have a layer of marshmallow in between them. The cookie "sandwich" is then dipped in chocolate so that the entire cookie has a thin layer of chocolate around it.

BIOLUMINESCENT MUSHROOM HUNTING

I will never forget the night I was camping with a group of women and girls in Acadia National Park. We were exploring the woods at night when we came across bioluminescent mushrooms! They were pale green and glowing and absolutely stunning. What a treasure to find in the woods at night! You can search online for "list of bioluminescent mushrooms" to see if any grow anywhere near you. If so, take your kids on a night time mushroom hunt to see if you find any that glow in the dark.

FIREFLY CATCHING

There is something so magical about being outside on a hot summer night and seeing the flashing lights of fireflies all across a field. Fireflies are gentle insects and relatively easy to capture. Here are some tips on catching fireflies, but please make sure to release them soon after capture. Like any wild animal, they are not happy in captivity.

1. First and foremost, make sure you are in an area where there are fireflies. Although fireflies are found throughout the world, they do not live everywhere.

2. Thoroughly clean and dry a glass jar with a lid.

3. Put several holes in the jar lid—put the lid over a piece of thick cardboard or towel and then hammer a nail through the lid in several places to make the holes.

4. Take your jar outside on a hot summer night and watch for fireflies.

5. Add a little bit of grass to the jar so the fireflies have cushioning.

6. If you see a flashing firefly then walk toward it. The light will flash on and off so don't be surprised if you have to take a few steps and then wait until it flashes again to know where to follow it. Keep following the flashing light until the firefly is in front of you.

7. When you get close to the firefly's location, put your jar down and take the lid off.

8. Wait for the firefly to flash again so that you can see where it is. Try to pick it up as gently as possible by scooping your hands around it.

9. If you are able to hold it, then bring it over to your jar and drop it gently inside.

10. See how many fireflies you can capture!

11. Keep your fireflies for an hour or so. Bring them into your home or tent and use them as a "lantern." My experience with fireflies is that if you set them down somewhere and just leave them alone, they will start to flash again.

12. Make sure to release the fireflies after an hour or so.

FIREFLY TALKING

Again, you need to make sure you are in or near a firefly habitat for this activity. Give your child a flashlight at night and let them "talk" to the fireflies. Your child can observe the pattern of flashing that a firefly makes. Then your child can respond to the firefly with the same flash pattern. This is a brief activity but well worth it. My son used to love this ritual just before bedtime—he would sit at the window and flash a pen light back and forth with fireflies. What a wonderful way to go to bed each night!

OWL WALK

If owls live in your area, an evening walk along a woodsy trail can be an enjoyable way for children to listen and watch for owls. You can prepare ahead of time by researching which owls live in your area, as well as what their calls sound like. This will help you and your kids better identify the owls if you spot them.

FULL MOON WALK

Walking at night during a full moon is enjoyable for kids because they can actually see at night. Full moon walks can be a family tradition or a one-time event—either way your kids can enjoy the fun of getting outdoors just before bedtime and letting go of some energy.

MOTH FEEDING

Moths tend to love sugary substances, so here is a way to make a snack for them. Make the snack, hang it outdoors, then wait until night time to go outside and see how many are eating. You may find other late-night snackers as well, such as beetles.

Materials:

- ⅛ cup of organic cane sugar (not beet sugar).

- Water.

- Three cotton balls.

- Three pieces of string about 1 ft (30 cm) long.

- An outdoor light.

Directions:

1. Dissolve the sugar in ¼ cup water.

2. Tie string around each cotton ball. Make sure the string is tied tightly.

3. Dip the cotton ball in the sugar mixture and then gently squeeze—you want the cotton ball to be moist but not dripping wet.

4. At sunset, hang the cotton balls from a light or lamp post outdoors.

5. Turn the outdoor light on.

6. When it gets dark, the moths will be attracted to the light and then find the food on the cotton balls.

MOON SHADOWS

Go outside on a clear night when there is a full moon and make Moon Shadows with the kids. You can even play a game of Shadow Tag if the moon is high enough in the sky. See page 173 for Shadow Tag instructions.

LEARNING TO RESPECT NATURE

I have always thrived in the outdoors. To me, being outside is the ultimate freedom and adventure. I grew up climbing trees, exploring, and in general awe of how amazing our world is. Now I'm lucky enough to watch my children follow that same path.

We live in town and have very little outdoor space, but we are fortunate to have a national park and the Atlantic Ocean within walking distance. When my children are outside, they are nearly overwhelmed by the mysteries and wonders of the great outdoors. They find grasshoppers, newly sprouted vegetable plants in our tiny garden, ripening cherries on our little fruit tree, or witness one of the bald eagles that live on a nearby island fly overhead while being chased by noisy crows.

Nature play is a large part of my family's lives because it is extremely important to instill in my children a feeling of reverence for the natural world. Our society is far too preoccupied with commercialism and material possessions. Nature play provides a respite from that, as well as infinite opportunities for discovery and wonder. I want my girls to feel deep respect for our planet and the life it sustains. And with that respect will hopefully come the desire to nurture and protect what is sacred and irreplaceable.

Kirsten Hardy
Parent of two young children

Figure 6.18 Kirsten's daughters have grown up enjoying nature-based play
Photo source: Hardy

Chapter 7

BLACKTOP ACTIVITIES

Blacktop refers to paved areas where children play, such as school playgrounds, sidewalks, paved driveways, and playing courts. Some children get little exposure to the typical places we think of as natural spaces, such as fields and forests, but blacktop does provide a common space for children to play outdoors.

SAFETY FIRST

When children are playing in paved areas make sure they are safe from vehicle traffic (e.g. parking lots are generally not a safe playing space for children).

- If children are playing on a paved driveway, make sure the driveway is blocked to oncoming traffic—it may help to park a car at the end of a driveway to block cars from pulling in.

- Make sure children wear shoes to protect their feet in paved areas. Pavement can heat up quickly, so make sure the surface is a safe temperature for kids to play on.

INTERACTIVE CHALK LANDSCAPES

Blacktop is akin to a giant canvas for kids with colored chalk. You can draw, play games, create new worlds, and interact with the art you create.

Castle chalk scene with a dragon's lair

Draw a castle with a dungeon, turret, stairs, and/or a large courtyard. The castle could also have a moat around it if you like. Then draw a dragon's lair a little distance away from the castle. Let your child pretend to be someone who lives in the castle, protects the castle, or is the dragon. They can run back and forth between the castle and the lair. If there is more than one child around they can take turns as different characters.

Superhero chalk scene

Draw a cityscape with different areas of the city needing help or rescue. Is the bakery out of cupcakes? Is there a cat stuck on the library roof? Is there a broken fire hydrant on the sidewalk? Brainstorm some kid-friendly emergencies your child can fix as a superhero. You could even draw a phone booth and put a towel or pretend cape there. Your child can run to the phone booth, tuck the towel in their shirt, and then zoom from one rescue to the next.

For added fun, draw clouds over the city skyline. Now your child can pretend to fly over the city to find where they are needed most. Then it's "off to the rescue!"

Under and over the sea chalk scene

Draw an ocean with a giant pirate ship floating on waves. Add pirates, a sea monster, a mermaid, a giant octopus, a submarine, or a lantern fish. The child can interact with all of the characters in imaginative play.

Race track chalk scene

Draw a large, circular race track. Your child can then pretend to be a racing car and zoom around the track. You can add a "muddy area," "sharp corner," "pit stop," "refueling station," or "oil slick" as obstacles for added challenges.

Treasure island chalk scene

Draw a large island with a pathway leading through dangerous obstacles to a "hidden treasure." Draw areas of quicksand, poisonous snakes, scorpions, rickety bridges, and hidden traps. Kids might also enjoy an added trading post where they trade pebbles and sticks (pretending they are food or tools).

3D CHALK DRAWINGS

This is a challenging activity that has much more appeal for the older kids. They can create block letters that look like they are "popping" out of the pavement, or create a scene that looks like something is coming out of the blacktop, or going into it.

Figure 7.1 3D Chalk Drawing of a man climbing out of the sidewalk—artwork by Destination ArtSwarm

CHALK PHOTO BOOTH

Have the child draw pictures with chalk that they can then lie next to or interact with for photo taking (remember, the child will need to lie or sit on the pavement in order to make it look like they are part of the picture). The child can draw things they might hold onto, like an ice cream, magic wand, umbrella, baseball bat, or sword. The child can also draw things that they are running away from, like a monster, or a lightning bolt. Tell the child to think of other objects or characters they can draw to interact with. If you have a camera, capture photos of the child interacting with their drawings.

Figure 7.2 Flying on the back of a giant bird created out of chalk

RAIN SILHOUETTES

Rain Silhouettes are made when an object on the ground keeps that space dry while water makes the ground wet all around it. If you lift the object, after the water has fallen, there will be the dry shape of the object left behind on the tar. Kids can purposely make shapes using this technique. A driveway and a basketball court are examples of blacktop spaces where you can try this activity.

Although "rain" is in the title of this activity, you can actually use a garden hose or watering can if you have one. These watering tools can be used in place of a rainstorm.

- Option 1: Find objects from the house or yard that can get wet. Lay these objects down on the pavement. Cookie sheets, pots, garden tools, plastic toys, and even large sticks or stones work well for this activity. Frisbees can be used to make polka dots. As the rain falls, the objects will get wet. However, depending on the shape and size of the object, the ground beneath will stay dry. When the rain stops, have the child lift the objects from the blacktop to see what shapes the objects left behind. The child can experiment to find out which objects create the best shapes.

- Option 2: If the child is very patient, *they* can be the object on the pavement. The child only needs to lie still on the pavement for a few moments as it starts to rain to get the desired results. Then they can stand up and look at the dry silhouette they left behind. This is especially fun with groups of children. Kids can get creative and silly, experimenting with different poses to see how their silhouettes turn out.

- Option 3: Use a hose to create a rain effect instead of waiting for a rainstorm.

- Option 4: Use laminated paper shapes instead of objects. The laminated paper shapes need to be anchored down by stones or other weights. If a parent or care provider has access to a laminator, then they can custom-make letters to spell out words (e.g. the child's name) or create multiple shapes of the same design (e.g. hearts and stars).

COLOR BRICKS

If you are in an area that has a sidewalk or wall made of bricks, the child can color the bricks different colors. In some cases you may need to ask permission to do so (i.e. if it is on the side of a building not owned by you). Color the bricks in rainbow colors or make smiley faces on every other brick. Get creative and make the bricks colorful and fun.

Figure 7.3 Coloring bricks every color of the rainbow

NATURE-BASED URBAN ART

Most blacktop, concrete, and other paved areas will have cracks and crevices that occur from wear and tear. These tiny spaces are perfect for filling with patterns and designs with found objects! Find natural materials in the area, such as acorns, acorn caps, pebbles, weeds, and sticks. Then use these objects to make lines, spirals, or other designs inside the crevices. You could use just one material (e.g. lining up sticks inside a crack). Or you could alternate materials to make designs and patterns (e.g. using sticks to make lines in one area and then acorn caps to make circles in another).

Another one of my favorite urban art forms is when people combine art with pre-existing structures, objects, or phenomena. For example, a person might see ivy growing over a brick wall and then draw a woman's face below it, to create the look that the ivy is her hair. Or another person might see a valve coming out of a wall and draw a man's face around it, making it look like the valve is a pipe coming out of his mouth. When using chalk, the artwork is temporary and harmless but you may still need to ask permission to create this type of art if it is on privately owned property.

HOPSCOTCH AND OTHER BLACKTOP GAMES

Don't forget the traditional blacktop games such as hopscotch and four square. If you are bringing kids to a blacktop area, go to your local library ahead of time and check out a book on blacktop games, or research such games online. Hand the kids some chalk and let them experiment with these different games.

Chapter 8

SAND AND BEACH

Lakes, ponds, river banks, and the ocean provide beaches where kids and care providers can enjoy a variety of play activities from swimming to beach combing and building sand castles.

SAFETY FIRST

- Children need to be supervised by adults and/or a lifeguard at *ALL* times when near the water.

- Make sure the kids in your care are wearing protective, waterproof sunscreen if needed.

- Use your discretion when it comes to footwear at a beach—some beaches have debris and litter that is not safe for bare feet.

- If you are bringing food items to an ocean beach, keep them in a cooler or safe spot—seagulls are experts at stealing unattended food.

SAND SCULPTURES

The key to creating sand sculptures is having sand that is wet enough to stay packed together. Wet sand is usually found closer to the water's edge or right after a high tide (if you are at the ocean). Kids can use beach buckets to transport wet sand as needed.

Directions:

1. Decide what you would like to create. A mermaid? A dinosaur? A cat? A princess? A racing car?

2. Start making piles of wet sand in the shape of your object. For example, if you are making a racing car, make a larger pile of

sand in the shape of the body of a car. Then add two or four smaller piles of wet sand where the tires will need to be.

3. Pat the sand down. Pat lightly so the sand doesn't crumble and fall. If the shape of your object needs to be adjusted, add or remove sand as needed to sculpt the correct shapes.

4. When you feel that the sculpture's shape is done, start adding details to it. You can use found pebbles, sticks, or shells to add these details. You can also use a stick or rock to "draw" lines into the sculpture as well. Just make sure you use gentle pressure though if drawing anything into your sculpture. Too much pressure could make the sculpture collapse.

Figure 8.1 A person sculpted out of sand
Photo source: Davis

EDGE OF THE TIDE SCULPTURES AND DRAWINGS

Build a castle, structure, or sand sculpture near the water's edge at the beach. You can also write a message in the sand or draw a picture there. As the tide comes in, watch as the waves wash it away. Kids can also have contests to see which structure or picture washes away first (or last).

Figure 8.2 A sculpture built at the edge of the tide
Photo source: Pastorelli

SAND CASTLES

Sand castles require wet sand in the same way that sand sculptures do. Although plastic sand castle molds can be helpful for building sand castles, they are certainly not necessary.

Figure 8.3 Building sand castles at the beach
Photo source: Vlachos

Directions:

1. Make piles of damp sand where you would like your castle towers to be. Pat and mold the towers into shape. It helps to pat gently because any pressure on the sand makes it likely to collapse.

2. If you would like walls in between the castle towers, you can put handfuls of wet sand where you would like the walls to be. Then use your fingers to pat and/or pinch the walls into shape.

3. You can use a stick to press down on the tops of the towers and walls to make indents in the sand. This will make the classic battlements pattern that kids often draw on castles.

4. Use sticks, rocks, shells, and sea glass to create windows, door frames, and rooflines.

5. You can also dig a moat around the castle if you like. Depending on how wet or dry the sand is, your moat might actually even be able to hold water in it. Bring water to your moat using a bucket or water bottle. Pour water in and see if the water will stay. If the water seeps into the sand, then you can fill the moat with pebbles or shells as a substitute for water.

PICTURES IN THE SAND USING FOUND OBJECTS

A sandy beach is a blank canvas. Have your child draw large pictures in the sand using a stick like a giant pencil. They can also drag their feet or toes in the sand, or use fingers as their drawing tools. Once the drawing is done, your child can collect objects from the beach to add to their drawing. It is best to encourage children to only collect natural objects such as driftwood, sticks, seaweed, shells, and pebbles so that they are not also collecting litter or undesirable items.

Pebbles, for example, can be added to a picture of a face for eyes, nostrils, teeth or freckles. Seaweed can be used for mustaches, monster tails, or mermaid hair. Sticks can be used for hair, dinosaur spikes, mohawks, and rays of a sun. See what your child can find to enhance and embellish their sand drawing.

Figure 8.4 This squid is squirting ink, represented by seaweed

SILLY SHADOW PORTRAITS

Figure 8.5 Silly Shadow Portrait on the beach

Many people choose to head to the beach on sunny days, and sunny days are perfect opportunities for making shadows. Making Silly Shadow Portraits is a two-person activity so you will either need to help the child with this project, or the child will need a friend to help out.

Have the child stand with their back against the sun and see where their shadow falls. Where the shadow of their head falls, draw a silly expression where the face would be or draw a crown for the head. You can also add other accessories and extras including tails, horns, mohawks, wings, scales, and so on. Kids enjoy creating these silly portraits of each other. The "portraits" are great photo opportunities too, so if you have a camera, bring it along to capture these fun portraits.

SHADOW TAG

Shadow Tag is a simple game where you try to step on someone's shadow while they try to step on yours. It's as easy as that. This game tends to send children into fits of giggles as they "step on your head" and "step on your hand," and so on. Another version of Shadow Tag is where you chase the players until you step on one of their shadows. That person then becomes "it" and has to chase other players until they can step on someone else's shadow.

DRAGON TAILS AND MERMAID HAIR

Seaweed that has washed up on the beach can be fun for dressing up and accessorizing at the beach. Tuck a string of seaweed in your child's back pocket or swimsuit to make a long tail. Or pile some on your child's head to make crazy mermaid hair. Seaweed quickly becomes a scarf, a leash, a beard, a sea dragon's tail, and more.

HANGMAN, HOPSCOTCH, AND TIC TAC TOE

Find a stick or small rock to draw a hangman, hopscotch, or tic tac toe (noughts and crosses) game on the beach. Kids can use pebbles and shells as tic tac toe pieces, or use a rock or shell as their hopscotch piece.

BEACH TEEPEE

Tall sticks can be leaned together to create a teepee on the beach. This project works best when you are at a beach where there are many large sticks available (e.g. a riverfront beach or lakeside beach). This project also works best if you have two or more people.

Directions:

1. Try to find sticks that measure about 6 ft (1.8 m) tall—you will want the sticks tall enough so you have room to sit inside the teepee. It will also be easier to build a teepee if some or all of your sticks have forked or "Y"-shaped tops, or have branches coming off of them. Sticks with these shapes will provide added support for your structure and be much easier to build.

2. Draw a square in the sand about 5 ft × 5 ft (1.5 m × 1.5 m). At each corner of the square, push a stick into the ground, but angle the sticks so that the tops are leaning toward the center of the square.

3. If the tops of the sticks have a forked- or "Y"-shaped top, lean another stick (or two) into the notch of that stick.

4. Decide which side of the square will be the opening to the teepee.

5. Place sticks evenly along the remaining three sides of the square, making sure each stick is angled to lean toward the center as well.

6. This part of the teepee process requires some manipulating till it works, but see which sticks can interlock with other sticks by using the notches and forked branches to lean against, and into, each other.

7. Remember to keep one side semi-open so that you can crawl inside.

8. Keep testing the integrity of the teepee by seeing if you can move any of the sticks easily. If any sticks are loose, try placing them in another position where they can interlock with another branch. Continue with this step until the teepee feels stable and strong enough for you to climb in the opening without it falling over or apart.

9. Have an adult double-check the structure for safety before sitting and playing in it.

BEACH BAKERY OR BISTRO

If you have any old pots and pans you are not using anymore or do not need, repurpose them by bringing them to the beach on a cool day where your child can create a beach bakery or bistro. Muffin tins can be filled with sand and decorated with shells and stones to look like cupcakes and muffins. Cookie sheets can hold sculpted sand cookies that have been decorated with seaweed and shells. Pots can be filled with water and filled with grasses for pasta, or mixed with stones and shells for soups. Let your child pretend to be a chef or baker and see what they cook for you. Make sure you use these only on a cooler day as the pots and pans heat up quickly in the sun.

HUM FOR A PERIWINKLE

Did you know you can entice a periwinkle snail out of its shell by humming to it? I am not sure if this works with any other kind of snail or shelled creature but in New England this is a charming rite of passage for coastal children. The trick is in the technique.

Directions:

1. Find a live periwinkle snail.

2. Hold your hand out flat, palm side up, and place the periwinkle on your hand. I usually place the periwinkle in the center of my palm or near the base of my fingers.

3. Now rest your chin on the base of your hand. You will feel like you are eye to eye with the periwinkle.

4. Now hum a song. The vibration of your voice will reverberate through your hand and entice the periwinkle to come out of its shell. Some snails are shyer than others but if you hum a little song and be patient, it will come out to say hello. Most kids find this enchanting and it's very endearing to find a child on the beach humming to a periwinkle.

POP SEAWEED

Rockweed seaweed is nature's equivalent of bubble wrap. The seaweed pods swell into bubble-like orbs and they pop when you squeeze them. If you live in a coastal area where rockweed grows, go on a search for this type of seaweed and try popping some with your fingers.

Figure 8.6 Rockweed seaweed—you can pop it

SQUIRT CLAMS

If you live in an area where clams burrow at the beach, then kids can try hunting for them. Clams are kid magnets because when you pick a clam out of the sand, they often squirt you (or someone else). The tricky part is digging for the clams to find them. In New England the tell-tale sign of clams are the tiny air holes they leave in the sand. Dig deep below and you might be lucky enough to find a clam. If that is the case, pull the clam out of the sand and hold it up. If the neck of the clam is sticking out, it just might squirt!

STRIPED STONE CIRCLES

Collect several beach stones that have a natural ring around them. Then see if you can connect the rings to make a circle. Can you make other shapes or even "draw" a picture with the lines in the stones?

Figure 8.7 An example of a Striped Stone Circle

BEACHCOMBING

Children are natural collectors and the beach can be a treasure trove of interesting finds. Here are some items that kids can collect from the beach: stones, shells, driftwood, sea glass, and sand dollars. Sand dollars are an echinoderm. Their shells are round and flat like coins.

Some collections are easy to preserve and keep, such as rocks and sea glass. Other items may need to be washed, such as seashells. Encourage kids to collect items from the beach only if it is okay with the beach owner (some towns and municipalities have rules saying "no removing items from the beach") and only if the collected item is not alive (i.e. leave live periwinkles, sea urchins, and crabs at the beach). Once the items are home, wash them if necessary and then find a special place for them.

- Collections can be placed in jars on a shelf or windowsill for decoration.

- Collections can be placed on a table designated for the child's learning about nature and science.

- Collections can be placed in an accessible container for the child to use for self-soothing and sorting. Many children love to sift through rocks and shells and sort them by shape, size, color, and interest.

- Some children enjoy collecting a small jar of sand from each beach they visit, and then labeling the jar with the name of the beach. Kids can compare sand from one beach to the next. Or, if the child visits one or two beaches in a lifetime, the jar of sand can be an endearing memento from their visit to the ocean.

- In the same tradition, children can bring home a special rock from each beach they visit. Use a permanent marker to write the name of the beach it came from and the date the child visited there.

- Collections can also be put aside for using in crafts later on.

BURY YOURSELF IN THE SAND

Children can bury their hands, feet, and most of their bodies in the sand on their own. However, many kids love to bury each other in the sand as a group activity. If your children want to bury each other in the sand, set some guidelines such as these:

- No putting sand near or around anyone's face.

- Only bury each other in horizontal positions, not vertical.

- Bury each other near adult supervision.

Figure 8.8 Buried in the sand

SAND ANGELS

Lie in the sand on your back. Then move your arms and legs out and in, as if you were doing jumping jacks (but lying down). It's just like making a snow angel but in the sand!

SAND SILHOUETTES

Figure 8.9 Polka dots on the beach

Lay any object on wet sand and then sprinkle dry sand over it to make Sand Silhouettes. When you lift the objects, the silhouette of the shape is left behind. My three favorite Sand Silhouettes to make are 1) people making funny poses lying down, 2) using Frisbees to make polka dots all over the wet part of a beach, and 3) making patterns with an object (e.g. using a lunch box to make a "brick wall" pattern).

You can also use poster board to make sand silhouettes.

Directions:

1. Cut a shape from the center of the poster board.

2. Lay the poster board on the wet sand.

3. Sprinkle dry sand over the poster board.

4. Lift the poster board carefully and carry it over to another area where you can brush the extra sand off.

5. Repeat as needed to make fun designs and patterns! We used this method to make the beach look like it had polka dots on the sand.

Chapter 9

FOREST AND TREES

CLIMBING TREES

Figure 9.1 Climbing trees

Explore this childhood rite of passage at least once. Let your child explore and climb a tree and with any luck they'll find a branch to sit on where they can read a book, have a snack, sketch a picture, daydream, spy on a sibling, and observe nature.

MAPLE SEED HELICOPTERS

Maple trees drop their seeds in spring and these seeds make great "helicopters" to fly. Simply hold a maple seed above your head or from a high place and then let go of it. The seed will spin in the wind as it falls to the ground.

Have contests to see whose maple seed can stay in the air the longest or travel the furthest.

Figure 9.2 Maple seeds look like this. They are also one of the seeds that look like fairy wings in the "Fairy Wings" activity on page 193

MAPLE SEED NOSES AND BEARDS

Maple seeds that are still green can be used to make silly noses and beards. Take a maple seed in your hand and break it in half (maple seeds have two sides, with the stem in between each side). Use your fingernail to peel apart the bottom of the seed where it was attached to the stem. The maple seed is slightly sticky in the center, which means it acts a little bit like glue. Attach the seed to the end of your child's nose, or see if you can get it to adhere to your child's chin. Kids can also try to see how many they can attach to their noses.

Figure 9.3 A maple seed nose
Photo source: King

LEAF CROWNS

Many children love to make and wear crowns. They can pretend they are kings or queens, fairy godmothers or fairy godfathers, masqueraders, jesters, or wearing party crowns.

Materials:

- Several collected leaves.
- Scissors.

Directions:

1. Make sure some of the leaves have long stems (e.g. maple leaves).

2. Use scissors to snip off pieces of leaf stems about 2 in (5 cm) in length. These pieces will be the "connectors."

3. Hold two leaves in your hand. Place one leaf overlapping the other, but not completely covering it.

4. Use one of the connector stems to poke a hole through the two leaves where they overlap.

5. Bend the connector stem downward and poke another hole for the connector to go through. The connector stem should now be holding the two leaves in place.

6. Continue connecting leaves together in this manner until the leaves are long enough to wrap around the child's head.

7. When the crown is the length needed, close the crown by connecting the first and last leaves together with a final connector stem.

Leaf crowns are not just for children, however. Try making leaf crowns for their favorite dolls and stuffed animals, too.

Figure 9.4 This lion from Laurie Made on Etsy looks royal in his leaf crown

LEAF CHAINS AND GARLANDS

Use the same method as above to create a long leaf garland. You can use leaf garlands to decorate a special play area in the forest. For example, string garlands from one tree to the next or hang a few from the same tree branch to create a "wall" or natural screen. You can also use leaf garlands for decorating at outdoor (and even indoor) parties.

Figure 9.5 This is how the stems work as "connectors" to make the leaf chain

TREE ART

Create art in the forest with tree trunks and sticks.

Figure 9.6 Sticks are placed between two tree trunks to create a pattern

Materials:

- Two trees close together or a tree with two trunks close together.

- Collected sticks of various sizes.

Directions:

1. Gather sticks and twigs that are about the same width as the space between the tree trunks.

2. Hold a stick between the tree trunks—slide the stick down or up until you find a spot where it fits. Push down a little on the stick to push it firmly in place. You may need to discard some of your sticks if they are too short. If they are too long, you can try to break off the sizes that you need.

3. See how many of your sticks can fit between the trees.

4. For an added challenge, once you have completed as many horizontal rows as possible, go back and fill in the spaces between the sticks with vertical rows—this step will use much smaller sticks.

5. Can you create other designs or patterns between the trees, using only sticks?

DECORATED TREE FORMATIONS

If you come across a tree that has an odd formation in the bark or trunk (e.g. a knot, hole, or tear that has healed), then challenge your child to see if they can create a pattern inside the formation, using natural materials. For example, use pine cones to create a sunburst shape in a tree hole, or use a horizontal line of twigs to fill a tear in the trunk.

WILLOW BRANCH CROWNS

Willow trees have pliable branches which can be easily molded into wreaths and crowns. Use clippers to remove some branches from a willow tree. Take a few branches and braid, twist, and/or weave them so they are intertwined. Wrap the branches around the wearer's head to gauge how long you will need the branches to be in order to reach around the child's head. When you have the desired length needed, secure the ends of the branches with a thinner willow branch (some are pliable enough to tie knots with) or tie the ends with string or yarn. Double check to make sure the crown will stay in place and that knots are secured. The child can now find flowers, feathers, or leaves to tuck into the crown and then wear it on their head.

APPLE FACES

Wild apple trees provide multiple opportunities for play, from climbing the tree to eating and playing games with the apples. A rather impish activity to do with wild apples is to bite faces onto the apples (silly faces, happy faces, monster faces, etc.) and leave the apple faces for someone else to find. Apple faces can be stacked or placed in tree nooks or knot holes, or lined along a long branch. Kids will find it humorous to imagine an unsuspecting passerby coming across these silly faces.

Figure 9.7 Apple faces resting in a tree

ACORN-CAP FINGER PUPPETS

Children can have impromptu forest puppet shows with these instant finger puppets.

Figure 9.8 Create these capped characters using acorns

Materials:

- Acorn caps.
- Felt-tip pen.

Directions:

1. Ask the child to gather acorn caps. The most obvious place to look for acorn caps is under an oak tree.

2. Draw funny faces on the child's fingertips.

3. Put acorn cap "hats" on her fingertips. Now you have finger puppets!

LEAF PILE JUMPING

Figure 9.9 Having fun jumping and playing in leaf piles
Photo source: Heather Mladek Photography

Have the kids rake or push a bunch of leaves together in a pile to jump into. Remind children ahead of time to make sure there is no debris in the leaves before making piles (such as the rake or litter). Kids can also bury each other up to their necks in the leaves.

PATHWAYS IN FALLEN LEAVES

If you come across a large space where leaves have fallen (such as a park or a lawn), then have the child walk through the leaves to create pathways. If you have more than one child, they can play "Follow the Leader" through the leaves or help to kick leaves aside to create cleaner looking pathways.

FAIRY WINGS

Maple seeds and other tree seeds fall from the tree and then land on the ground. As time goes on, the plant material decomposes around the seed until the plant veins remain and are held together in the shape of the maple seed (which just so happens to look like fairy wings). Kids can look for fairy wings under and around maple trees from late fall through the winter. It is especially magical for children to find these fairy wings resting on top of the snow in winter.

FOREST TREASURES

Children can find natural objects to collect from trees and forests, such as pine cones, acorns, leaves, and sticks. These materials can be used in crafts or stored at home for decoration.

If you are going to keep the acorns long term or use them in crafts, you will need to clean and heat them to make sure you do not bring any unwanted insects into the house.

Directions:

1. Clean the acorns with water and soap.

2. Dry the acorns with a towel and inspect them for holes. Discard any acorns with holes in them.

3. Spread the remaining acorns on a cookie sheet and bake them at the lowest setting of your oven (usually 175°F/80°C) for three hours. This will kill off insects and any mold or mildew.

4. Allow them to cool. Now they are ready for crafting or storing.

Chapter 10

FIELDS AND GRASSY AREAS

TUMBLE AND ROLL

Figure 10.1 Tumbling in the grass
Photo source: Heather Mladek Photography

Grass feels wonderful under bare toes and provides a natural carpet for fun outdoor play. Let your children tumble, roll, and explore in the grass. If you live near gentle grassy knolls, have your child roll down the hills.

FLOUR LAWN PICTURES

Materials:

- Large poster board.
- Flour (if your child is gluten sensitive, use cornmeal).

Directions:

1. Create a giant stencil. Cut a simple shape from the center of the poster board, such as a heart, star, or circle.

2. Lay the stencil in a flat area of the grass.

3. Sprinkle or sift the flour over the stencil to create a thin but visible layer.

4. Gently pick up the poster board stencil so as not to spill the excess flour that landed on the paper.

5. Walk with the stencil to a non-grassy area to tap the excess flour from the stencil.

6. Repeat this process to create as many shapes as you need on the grass.

FOUR-LEAF CLOVER HUNT

If clover grows in a grassy area nearby, send the children out on a four-leaf clover hunt. Four-leaf clovers are considered good luck! If a four-leaf clover is found, make sure you take a picture of it or preserve it if you can. To preserve it, lay it flat between two layers of tissue paper or wax paper and place it in a heavy book. Keep it stored in the book until the four-leaf clover is flat and dried out. You can continue to keep it stored in the book if you like, or you can use it in a craft project.

Figure 10.2 A four-leaf clover—how lucky
Photo source: Heather Mladek Photography

PATHWAYS IN THE FIELDS

If you are near a large field with tall grass, send the children on a walk through the fields to create "pathways and roads." The more they walk over these pathways, the more packed down and flat they will become. Kids can even stomp out areas in the grass for sitting or play areas. Once the pathways and areas are all packed down, kids will enjoy running and exploring through the spaces. Have them collect flowers as they go and then they can do the next activity—make flower chains!

FLOWER CHAINS

Kids can pick flowers with wide or sturdy stalks on them to create flower chains. Flower chains can be used to decorate an outdoor play area for the afternoon. If your child loves an outdoor picnic or tea party, then hang some flower chains nearby for added charm. They can also be hung from tree branches or laid on the ground to create a boundary.

Directions:

1. Pick several flowers that have strong stalks on them (e.g. dandelions, daisies, and clover). Keep the stems attached. You will need a few inches of stem for each flower.

2. Use your fingernail to cut a small opening in the stem of the flower. Make this cut a little below the flower head.

3. Slide another flower stem through this hole you just created.

4. Keep repeating these steps until you have the length of chain you need.

5. Hang or drape the chain as desired. If some flowers slip out of the stems, simply re-insert the flowers. Sometimes the stems will rip or tear, in which case you need to put in a replacement flower.

FLOWER CROWNS

Follow the directions for making a flower chain. When the chain gets to be a few flowers long, test the length of it around your child's head. Add flowers as needed to make it fit your child's head. When you have the right length, put the last flower stem through the first flower's stem. This will close the loop in the crown and should fit on your child's head.

For added durability you can always use field grasses to tie the stems into place. The grass will need to be green or fresh grass so that it is strong and supple enough to tie with.

Figure 10.3 Wearing a flower crown

CATTAIL PLANTS SWORDS

Cattail plants grow in wet areas, typically near swamps or ponds. They are a tall plant that resembles a thick stalk of grass with a cigar or corndog speared at the top. The top is what contains the seeds, and if you tear this seedy area apart, you will have an abundance of fluffy seeds everywhere. The explosive seed mess is a kid magnet—you have been forewarned!

Children can break off a cattail toward the bottom of the stalk and pretend the stalk is a sword. When they hit their cattail sword against a rock or other object, the seeds from the cattail will start to disperse. Depending on the season, the cattail may not burst open easily (early in the cattail season) or it may appear to burst or explode (if late in the season). Regardless, cattail sword fighting is a fun play activity for many children.

SEED POD COLLECTING

In the fall, as flowers have started to die and "go to seed," you can find many seed pods for collecting. The types of pods you find will depend on your climate. However, have your child explore and see what kinds of pods they can find. Seed pods can be set aside for craft projects and creative play. For example, milkweed pods can be used to make fairy boats or miniature houses. Some seed pods are beautiful works of art in their own right and make whimsical additions to a child's collection of natural treasures.

Chapter 11

PUDDLES AND MUD

Rain puddles and mud provide creative play opportunities for your children. Kids do not need raincoats and boots to enjoy playing in the mud or puddles—they can enjoy this messy play in their bare feet and a set of old clothes. You can also go on "mud walks" with your kids to explore the mud and splash in puddles.

PUDDLE JUMPING

Rain puddles and mud provide creative play opportunities for your children. Allow kids to explore puddles after a rainfall. They can walk through the puddles, splash in them, swish their feet in them, play with water toys in them, and play with sticks in them too. You can also go on a family "mud walk" with your kids to explore what mud is like. Write messages and draw pictures in the mud along the way.

Figure 11.1 Walking through a giant puddle

Figure 11.2 Exploring on a mud walk

PUDDLE TRACING WITH CHALK

If you find a puddle on a blacktop or sidewalk, trace the outer edges of the puddle with chalk. As the day goes on, or as days pass (depending on your climate), observe how the puddle shrinks in size as the water evaporates. (The chalk outline will remind your child of the size of the puddle before it evaporated.)

RIVER MAKING

Large mud puddles can be reshaped to create a river landscape. If you drag your foot or a stick from the edge of the puddle, the water in the puddle will fill up that space. If you continue dragging the line, the water will continue to follow. The more you reinforce these little rivers by dragging an object over them, the more defined the river will be. See the next section for how to turn your rivers into a whole new water world.

MINIATURE WATER WORLD OR MARINA

Your child can use a puddle as a miniature marina or water world for boats and washable toys. If your child has washable figurines, then puddles (and the land surrounding the puddles) can become an imaginary world for their figurines to play in. Soldiers, dinosaurs, mud-loving princesses, animals, and vehicles can be placed all around the puddle in different lands. If the child has floating toys such as boats, the figurines can travel from one side of the puddle to the other to explore new lands, trade, or visit friends. If your child has made rivers, as mentioned above, then the world of many lands is extended and the child can add even more "lands" for their figurines to play in.

CONSTRUCTION SITES AND TRUCK BATHS

Does your child have trucks and cars that are washable? If so, they can use puddles as part of a construction site. Toy dump trucks and bucket loaders are easy to fill with dirt, mud, and puddle water which can be transported from one side of the puddle to the other. Grader trucks can smooth out muddy areas so that other trucks and cars can drive over the mud. Allow your child to get messy and wet. When they are done playing with their trucks they can hose them down to wash them, or take them all to the "truck bath" station (provide some clean water to wash off the trucks).

ICE CUBE BOATS

Figure 11.3 Ice Cube Boats turned into pirate ships

Ice Cube Boats can be a cooling activity on a hot summer day. Kids make these tiny boats out of ice cubes ahead of time and then play with them in puddles.

Materials:

- Ice cube tray or small containers to freeze water.

- Water.

- Freezer.

- Toothpicks or small sticks.

- Masking tape.

- Leaves or paper.

- Acrylic paint or permanent markers (optional).

Directions:

1. Fill an ice cube tray or small plastic containers with water.

2. Place in the freezer.

3. When the water starts to freeze, poke a toothpick or small stick into the center of each ice boat. This will become the boat's mast. Note: This part of the activity is tricky as the mast may be difficult to keep upright. If that is the case, you can wait a little longer to insert the mast into the boat (when the water is more frozen), or you can use masking tape to create temporary "walls" for the toothpicks to lean against until the ice freezes.

4. Gather leaves that will fit the masts of your boats, or cut paper sails to size. If you want, you can paint the leaves with acrylic paint, but allow the paint to dry before going on to the next step. If you are making paper sails, then you can use permanent markers to decorate them.

5. When the ice cube boats are frozen, attach the sails—push the toothpick through the bottom of the sail and then bend the sail slightly so you can poke another hole for the mast to go through.

Now you can put your Ice Cube Boats in a puddle to see how they float! If you end up with tipsy boats this is a great opportunity to play pirate ships—pretend your boats have been struck by cannon fire and are sinking in the ocean. If you ended up with boats that float and remain balanced, then enjoy watching them sail around until they start to melt. You can even have races to see whose ice boat melts the fastest or lasts the longest.

MUD CAKES AND MUD PIES

The only ingredients you need for making mud cakes and mud pies are dirt and water. Provide your child with containers for outdoor "baking"—recyclables work beautifully for this project. If you have coffee cans, plastic containers, plastic egg cartons, or even coffee cups, set them aside for your child to use for mud baking. Your child can then use the containers to mix water with dirt to make mud. They can mix the mud with their hands or they can use sticks. However, if you do not have containers, that is okay. I never used them when I was a kid and I made plenty of cakes and pies by hand.

Additional tips for mud baking:

- Dry gravel and sand can be used as pretend cinnamon sugar, sprinkles, powdered sugar, and crumb topping.

- Pebbles can be used as pretend candies or cherries to decorate the tops of mud cakes.

- Sticks can be used as pretend birthday candles.

- Handfuls of grass can be broken up into little pieces to look like shredded coconut.

- Acorn caps can be used as nonpareils or decorative candies for the cakes.

- Seed pods can be used for decorations on a cake or pie.

"FOSSIL" DIG

If you have an abundance of mud in your yard or play area, have your child make a large mound of mud for this activity. They can use a shovel, bucket, or even their hands to create the mound. Next, have your child hide some sticks, rocks, beach shells, miniature toy dinosaurs, or other objects in the mud. Wait for the mud to dry—the timing of this step will depend on your climate.

When the mud is dry, your child can pretend to go on a fossil hunt in the dried mud. If your child has a spoon, shovel, fork, rock, or stick, she can chip away at the mud to find the hidden objects inside.

MUD BRICKS

Hand your child some empty ice cube trays and recycled plastic or lined containers (such as juice cartons and yogurt or apple sauce cups) and have your child pack mud into them. Set them aside outdoors until they have dried and hardened. Tap the bricks out and see if they maintained shape and integrity—some mud will break easily. If the bricks keep their shape, have your child build a structure with them. Build a house for a mud fairy, a stall for a horse, a garage for a car, or a mud bakery filled with mini mud pies.

Chapter 12

RIVERS AND STREAMS

Rivers and streams are magnets for imaginative children—they can wade, splash, explore, search for wildlife, walk across stones or fallen logs, and play among the river banks.

Water shoes can be helpful to protect your child's feet while wading and exploring rivers. However, if you know the area well enough to know it's safe underfoot, barefoot is a wonderful way to explore a river or stream. Rocks and soot are to be expected and are generally safe for bare feet. Fishing lures and other litter is not—if there is litter around, make sure your child has protected feet. Supervise young children near water at all times.

BRIDGE HUNT

Walk along the banks of a small river or stream and see if you can find any natural bridges. There are generally two types of natural bridges—trees that have fallen across the stream and rocks that create a natural walkway across the water.

Figure 12.1 Relaxing on a natural bridge

BOAT BUILDING

Make boats out of natural and found materials and send them down the river.

Figure 12.2 The base of the boat is made of driftwood, which is soft wood Toothpicks are easily inserted into the driftwood to create masts

Materials:

- Natural materials collected from your area, such as tree bark (use only bark that has fallen off the trees—do not strip bark from a tree as it can harm the tree), sticks, driftwood, acorns, pine cones, leaves, leaf stems, twigs, and grasses to create these boats.

- Wooden toothpicks (optional).

- Water-based natural clay (make sure to use natural-colored clay because you do not want dyes to get in the water).

- Twine or string.

- Scissors.

Directions:

1. Select a sturdy material for the bottom of the boat. Test it in the water before going any further—if it doesn't float, don't use it. (Bark and wide sticks typically work best, but experiment on your own to see what works for you.)

2. Choose a twig (alternatively, you can use a toothpick) and a leaf to create the mast and sail. Push the twig gently through the leaf. Poke another hole a little further away from the first hole. Fold the leaf up or down to bring the twig through the second hole. The twig should stay in place since it passes through both holes. Straighten the leaf out and adjust the twig and leaf as needed.

3. Place a small amount of clay on the bottom of your boat—about the size of a small gumball. Stick the mast into the clay. Add clay if needed to hold the mast in place but use as little clay as possible to keep the boat light.

4. Use twine or string to secure any pieces if needed.

5. See how it floats!

There will be times when you need to adjust your boat by finding a different size twig or leaf. You might also want to experiment with completely new designs. Once you get the hang of making boats, you can try using other materials such as seed pods or acorn caps.

POOH STICKS

Pooh Sticks is an activity that comes from A.A. Milne's book series about Winnie the Pooh and Christopher Robin. Pooh and Christopher Robin would stand on a small bridge that crosses a river or stream. They would drop a stick over one side of the bridge, then go to the opposite side of the bridge to watch for the stick. You can also drop leaves into the water to watch them flow in the current.

DAM BUILDING

If you live near a small stream, challenge your child to build a temporary dam in the water. This is an activity that needs to be supervised by an adult since it is in the water.

Gather sticks, leaves, and other forest debris. You may even need rocks, depending on your design. Next, see if your child can block the water flow or even alter it. Can they make turns in the water? Can they make a mini pool? Can they stop the flow of water altogether? Kids can pretend they are beavers, engineers, and future architects as they reconstruct and redesign the water flow.

When your child is all done with this activity, have them return the water flow to normal since there are many life forms depending on the natural state of the water.

SALAMANDER, SNAIL, AND BUG HUNT

Rivers and streams offer rich opportunities for life. Many times there are animals and insects near streams that are not found anywhere else. Give your children the opportunity to explore a river's edge or stream to see what lives there and around the area. Look in the water, along the riverbanks, and near the surrounding area under rocks and logs.

Of course, be mindful of inherent risks and know what plants or animals are best avoided in your area—otherwise, go explore! It is delightful when children discover a centipede, toad, salamander, water bugs, or other creatures they have never seen up close before.

If your child loves to write or draw, bring along a nature journal for them to keep track of the places they explore and what they discovered.

Figure 12.3 Finding large snails in the water

SPLASH AND WADE

Many children naturally gravitate to water, begging to dip their toes in and splash around. Allow them this time to explore, play, and cool off.

Figure 12.4 Splashing around
Photo source: Guertin

Chapter 13

SNOW

Not everyone loves cold, snowy climates, but I certainly do. Snow provides the opportunity for outdoor play in many different forms, from sledding, skiing, and ice skating to snow sculptures, snow angels, and snowball fights. Snow creates a winter wonderland of fun.

SNOW SCULPTURES

In order to make snow sculptures of any kind, you need the right consistency of snow. It has to be "sticky" enough to hold together. Sometimes you will get sticky snow during a snowstorm and other times you have to wait for snow on the ground to warm up just enough to start melting a little. That is when it has the best texture for sculpting.

Many people think of "snowmen" as being the quintessential sculpture of winter, but you can really make just about anything out of snow. You can also create snow people in many shapes and sizes and performing many different actions. Let your child get creative with their ideas of what to build in the snow, but here are some ideas to get their imaginations started.

Figure 13.1 In between ice skating breaks, he built a snow person and rabbit to join him on the bench

SNOW PEOPLE

Challenge your child to make a snowperson doing one of the following:

- Standing on a doorstep, knocking at the door.
- Peeking in a window.
- Having a picnic.
- Looking up at the sky.
- Shoveling snow.
- Patting a snow dog.

Figure 13.2 A tiny snow person peeking in the window

SNOW INSECTS AND ANIMALS

If you want a little more challenge when it comes to playing in the snow, try creating an animal out of snow! You can try your hand at building any creature, from insects to giraffes. You might even be able to make a unicorn or dragon!

Suggestions for making snow insects and snow arachnids:

- To make insect bodies: Use small snowballs stacked on top of each other or placed side by side. A centipede or caterpillar will need many snowballs side by side to make the long body. An ant, spider, or butterfly will only need 2–3 snowballs to make the body.

- To make insect legs: Use thin sticks, dried grass stalks, reeds, or flower stems. For example, if you had a flower garden or ornamental grasses in your yard over the summer, you probably still have dried, brown remnants poking out of the snow. If not, try finding sticks. Sticks are easily taken from fallen branches in the woods.

- To make insect antennae: Use two pieces of dried grass or long slender leaves—poke the ends into the top of the head. If it's hard to get the grass or leaf stem into the insect's head, try creating the hole first, using a toothpick or stick. Then put the stem into the hole.

- To make other insect details: See what other natural materials you can find in your yard to make details such as wings, hair, and the hairy spikes you often see coming out of caterpillars' backs and tail ends. Seed pods, acorn caps, dried tufts of ornamental grasses, tiny pine cones, lichen, and seeds can all be used to add intriguing detail to your insect. For wings you can use dried seed pods (e.g. maple leaf seeds). You can also use shells from peanuts or another nut, pine cone seeds, pine needles, or dried leaves to create insect wings.

- Insect faces: Use seeds, tiny pebbles, and dried grasses to make insect faces. You can also just "draw" the face onto the insect by using your fingernail or a stick.

Suggestions for making snow animals:

Figure 13.3 A small cat made out of snow

- Animal body shapes: To create animal body shapes you will most likely need to combine a variety of different shaped snowballs. First you need to decide if your animal is going to be lying in the snow or standing. Lying animals can be created by making a large mound of snow and then sculpting the legs by adding just a little extra snow where the legs would rest. Standing animals can be created by making stacks of large sturdy snowballs for long legs, or small stacks of sturdy snowballs for smaller legs. Once the legs are done, the body gets added or sculpted. Then the neck and head go on top of the body. Each step requires the builder to assess the size and shape of each body part and to pack snow around all connecting parts.

- Animal fur and hair: Dried grasses, hay, straw, and even dog or cat hair from brushing your pets can be added to your snow creatures to make them look fuzzy and hairy.

- Quills and scales: Pine cones, pine cone seeds, flat stones, sticks, grass reeds, and dried stalks can all be poked into a snow sculpture to create quills or armored plates and scales.

- Fish and aquatic animals: Marine animals are most easily sculpted lying on their bellies in the snow. You can make a large mound of snow for the main body, then add snow in the places where fins, tails, or tentacles would go. You can also use a butter knife or stick (or other similar object) to "draw" lines or add details such as suction cups or scales. If your aquatic animal has bright colors you could also spritz it with water that has been dyed with food coloring. Simply mix water and food dye in a spray bottle and then spritz the color onto your sculpture.

- Birds: Whether you are building large birds of prey or small songbirds, you can start with the body and head. Make a larger oval shape for the body of the bird and a small but proportional snowball for the head. Actual feathers can be stuck into the sculpture if you have them. You can also create feathers and wings from dried leaves or swags of pine needles. Beaks can be created from dried grass reeds or flower stalks: Bend a piece of the grass or flower stem in half. If it stays in a "V" shape you can poke the two ends into the bird's face and the pointed end will stick out like a beak. Pointed rocks and pine cones are also good substitutes for beaks.

- Animal faces: Look around for pebbles, seeds, grasses, and other natural materials to create your animal faces. You can even use fruits and vegetables (including dried and dehydrated), dried legumes, and nuts/seeds from the kitchen as long as kids get adult permission first.

- Animal ears: You can usually sculpt what you need for ears out of snow. But for added detail, pine cones make great ears for animals such as dogs and horses.

- Animal tails: Snow can be sculpted to make small tails that belong to animals such as rabbits. Long tails can be made from tree branches (pine and fir branches work really well if you have access to them), dried grasses, a cat-o-nine tail, flower stalks (the ones with dried flowers still attached are fun tails for lions), and even seaweed.

FANTASY SNOW CREATURES

These snow creatures are especially challenging but well worth the effort! If your little sculptor has a lot of patience and endurance, then they might like to build one of the following mythical creatures.

Snow dragons

Make a snow dragon lying along the ground with its mouth open, or partially open. The body of the dragon is a large mound of snow, with sculpted mounds for the muscular legs. The tail can be built initially with a curving line of snowballs—larger snowballs toward the dragon's body and smaller snowballs toward the tip of the tail. Then snow can be packed in between and around the snowballs to smooth out the shape. The dragon's head can remain resting on the ground since it's easiest to build this way. Your child can take the creative freedom here to make a dragon's mouth full of teeth that can be made from icicles, ice cubes, or sculpted teeth. And if your child is able, have them create an opening in the mouth where they can put a battery tea light or even a glow stick for night time. This will make the dragon look like it has fire in its mouth.

Snow mermaid

Use mounds of snow to create the figure of a mermaid lying down. Dried leaves, stones, and twigs can be used to create a pattern of scales on the mermaid's tail. Dried grasses or pine needles can be used to make her hair.

Loch Ness snow monster

Whenever I think of the Loch Ness monster, I think of the quintessential long neck coming out of the water. I also think of two bumps protruding out of the water, followed by its tail. This kind of water monster is humorous to build if you live on or near a body of water that freezes really well (and deep) during the colder months.

To make your own Loch Ness monster, start with two large snow mounds spaced apart from each other. Then add a tail—you have creative license here to decide whether the tail is upright, or flowing in the "water." To make the head you can stack large to small snowballs, as if you were building a snowman, and then add an oblong snowball horizontally at the top to make the monster's head. However, you will want to pack just enough snow in between all the snowballs so that the neck looks smooth.

Finally, add the final details. Make snowballs and add them to the top of the mounds for scales. You can add snow to the snowballs to sculpt them into rounded triangle shapes if you like. Find small stones for the monster's eyes and use sticks for the outline of the eyes. From a distance it will look as if your sea monster is truly rising out of the frozen water.

SNOW FORTS AND IGLOOS

Figure 13.4 Peeking out of the window

Snow forts are one of my favorite winter activities because they are fun to build and you can use your fort for many adventures.

- Have a winter picnic in your fort.

- Have a candlelight dinner in your fort (if younger kids are present, you can use a well-protected lantern or battery light).

- Grab blankets at bedtime and head out to the fort for bedtime stories by lantern light.

- If your fort has no ceiling, then go stargazing from your fort—wrap up in warm blankets or sleeping bags and just lie on the fort floor to look up at the stars.

- Use the fort for protection during a snowball fight.

Following are suggestions for various types of snow forts and igloos, and how to build them.

Standard snow fort

Use a shovel to clear out a square shape in the snow. As you shovel, dump the snow along the perimeter of the square to create fort "walls." Make sure you leave one empty space along the wall for an entrance. Once the space inside the fort has been cleared, pack the snow along the walls by patting them down. This will make them sturdier. Next, make large snowballs (like the size you would use for the bottom of a snowperson) or snow blocks (using a snow block maker) to add to the wall. Pack snow in along any cracks of the bricks and in between. Continue to build up the walls until you have the desired height.

Extended snow fort

Instead of making a square-shaped fort you can add rooms to your fort. I think the biggest snow fort we built had four rooms to it but as you can guess, the more rooms you want the longer it takes to build it and you will need to have plenty of snow on the ground. The advantage to a fort with multiple rooms is that the child can designate a special purpose for each room and have more flexibility for pretend play.

Tree sardine forts

If you have a tree in your yard or play area that has more than two thick trunks to it, you can create a small but unique tree fort. Pack snow between the tree trunks to create walls between the trunks. If you have a few trees to build with, kids can make more than one tree fort and use the forts for snowball fights and hiding games. Tree Sardine Forts are usually very tight and just big enough for a child to stand or sit in, so if you need a stealth or well-hidden fort, then this fort is for you.

Igloo-building

For best results, purchase a plastic mold for making igloo blocks. The blocks are shaped with a slight angle and curve to them so that the walls create the classic igloo dome. The molds come with instructions for how to use them. Although a bit pricey and complex, building an igloo is a fun winter challenge.

Fort and igloo details

Figure 13.5 Ice windows and natural materials decorate this fort wall

Use grass, sticks, rocks, pine cones, and other natural materials to decorate the outside of your fort. For example, insert sticks along the top wall of your fort to make it look more like a fortress or medieval dungeon. You can also use a stick like a pencil and "draw" lines and details in the fort. You can draw doorways, windows, and bricks.

How about windows for your fort? Ice windows add unique and unexpected detail to your snow structures. To make them you will need baking pans or plastic containers.

Pour a thick layer of water into the pans or containers and place them outside to freeze. The length of time for your windows to freeze will depend on the outside temperature. When the windows are completely frozen, pop them out of the container and add them to your fort. If you already have a fort built, you should be able to cut out a space for your window to sit in.

Thankfully, this activity is pretty forgiving—if you cut out a space that is too large, then pack snow back into the space and try to place the window again. Add or remove snow as needed to get your window to sit in the wall.

If you wait for your windows to be made before building your fort, that is okay too. You just add your windows into the fort walls just as you would if they were a brick of snow. Add snow around the window edges and make sure to fill in any cracks and gaps with more snow.

Here are two tips for making windows:

1. If you want your windows to be clear, then boil the water before using it and make sure the child has an adult to help them with this step. If you do not boil the water first, your windows will be more white and cloudy looking.

2. If you want to add window grids, then wait until the windows are halfway frozen and then add sticks to the center grids of the windows. Allow them to finish freezing.

SNOW FURNITURE

Create a sculpture that you can actually sit or lie on. Here are some ideas:

- Build a giant king- or queen-sized throne.

- Sculpt a snow lounger or snow couch.

- Construct a snow table with snow benches around it. Sit down at your snow table for a snack or meal.

- Create a snow bed and then come out at night to lie on the bed in a sleeping bag to watch the stars.

PATHWAYS AND PATTERNS IN THE SNOW

Your child can use their stomping feet to create pathways and patterns in the yard. Make sure they're wearing a warm pair of boots and then challenge them to stomp out one of these shapes in the snow: circle, spiral, a path around the house, the shape of a letter, a pattern like checker squares, zig zags, or waves.

SNOW TUNNELS

Figure 13.6 Peeking out of a Snow Tunnel
Photo souce: Guertin

Snow Tunnels can be built in snow banks where snow has been piled high and packed well. A word of caution: Make sure your child always has supervision or a responsible buddy present when building tunnels (in case the tunnel collapses). Kids also need the buddy to keep watch for plow trucks and other vehicles that might come near the snow bank. Kids playing behind or in snow banks are often not visible to plow trucks so it's best practice always to have a buddy as a lookout.

To make a Snow Tunnel you want to create a passageway from one side of the snow bank to the other. A snow shovel comes in handy for this activity but an industrious and energetic child can create a tunnel without the need for any tools. Simply dig out a hole through the snow bank. At all times, make sure the tunnel is not going to collapse. This means making sure the top of the tunnel is not too heavy and not too weak. Make sure your child keeps an eye on the integrity of the tunnel as they build it.

Once the tunnel is complete, the child should be able to crawl through the tunnel and to the other side of the snow bank. If your child is claustrophobic or does not enjoy crawling through tunnels, they can also use the tunnel as a communication system or secret spy center. Kids can send secret messages through the tunnel or use it for hiding needed items such as snacks, water, or extra gloves. A secret tunnel also makes a perfect storage spot for a cache of snowballs.

SNOWBALL SCULPTURES

Snowballs can be used as a medium for creating outdoor sculptures. My son and I use an inexpensive snowball maker to make snowballs to use in sculptures because they come out perfectly smooth and round. However, you can also make the snowballs by hand. Here are some specific ideas for snowball sculptures:

Snowball trees

If you have any shrubs or bushes that have been pruned for the winter, then this project is quick, easy, and downright silly. Simply make your snowballs and attach them to the end of pruned branches. Your pruned tree or bush will look like it is growing snowballs.

Figure 13.7 A Snowball Tree

Snowball sculptures between tree trunks

Find a crack or wedge between tree trunks or in a structure that you can fill with snowballs. Depending on the size of the crack or wedge, the snowballs may need to be small or large. Create the size of the snowball according to the space it has to fill. Possible places to create wedged snowball sculptures are:

- In the wedge between two tree trunks from the same tree.

- In a crack of a brick or stone wall.

- In the holes of a chain link fence. You can actually create patterns, words, and images using snowballs in a fence.

Figure 13.8 Snowballs stacked between tree trunks

Snowball stacks

Have your child find creative places to stack some snowballs, or challenge them to see how many they can stack. Snowballs can be stacked on top of fence posts, along stone or cement walls, along snow fort walls, and along railings. Freestanding stacks can also be placed on the ground in random places or in a pattern (e.g. lining a walkway).

SNOWBALL FIGHT

Snowball fights are the quintessential winter activity and the concept is really quite simple—you make a snowball and you throw it at someone. Granted, it is best to have a snowball fight with a willing opponent and it's best to agree on the rules before throwing the first snowball. Most people agree that "no throwing snowballs at people's faces" is a good rule, but again, talk amongst your players and agree on the rules beforehand.

SNOW ANGELS

Figure 13.9 Making a Snow Angel

Freshly fallen snow is the best snow to use for making snow angels. After a snowfall, have your child lie in the snow and then move their arms and legs out, then in, then out again. Then, when they stand up and look down, they will see an angel shape in the snow. They can also create a face and decorate the rest of the angel with pebbles, grasses, or other natural materials if available.

SNOWFLAKES ON YOUR TONGUE

This classic rite of passage is short and sweet—simply go outside during a snowfall and have your child stick their tongue out to catch snowflakes.

SNOWFLAKES ON A DARK SURFACE

Snowflakes are absolutely stunning in design if you ever have the chance to look at them up close. Give your child a dark piece of fabric or thick paper to take outside during a snowfall. Put the fabric or paper on a flat surface and observe the snowflakes that fall onto it. A magnifying glass is not necessary but is certainly a bonus for looking at snowflakes more closely.

FROZEN BUBBLES

Take your bubbles outside during a cold winter day and see what happens when you blow bubbles. Depending on the temperature, the bubbles can take on interesting shapes and characteristics. If it is cold enough, you might even be able to watch a bubble freeze!

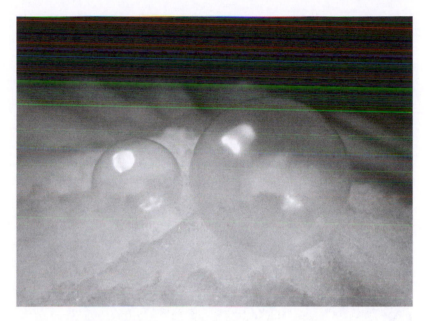

Figure 13.10 The bubbles start to freeze and turn into odd shapes

FROZEN PUDDLES

Frozen puddles provide a temporary, and therefore unique, opportunity for winter play. Here are some winter activities that kids can play on frozen puddles:

- Puddle skating: Have your kids keep their boots on and let them slip and slide on the puddles as if they are ice skating.

- Puddle stomping: Let your child stomp on the puddle until it cracks and crushes. This works best when the puddle is half frozen or has a thin layer of ice.

- Puddle hockey: Turn the puddle into a mini hockey rink. Create goals at each end of the puddle and then try to get a pebble in the goal.

- Puddle targets: Set up a target on the puddle, such as a stick or rock. Give each child an ice cube and then see which child can slide their ice cube closest to the target.

- Puddle bowling: Set figurines on the puddle and then use an ice cube or pebble to try to knock them down.

Always make sure you know the depth of a frozen puddle; there could be a drowning hazard if the ice breaks and there is deep water underneath.

ICY SNOW CARVING

Figure 13.11 A face carved out of icy snow

When snow cover becomes crusty and crunchy, you can cut it into various shapes and sizes. Simply use a butter knife to cut through the top layer of snow. Then carve the shape you need. Lift the shape out of the snow gently so as not to break it.

We have used rectangles and squares from icy snow to decorate fort walls. We have also created abstract art, props for snow people, and created ice lanterns using this technique.

ICE LANTERNS

Ice lanterns can be made a few different ways but we use the method above to make ours. These lanterns are for outdoor use only and are made on top of the snow. You can make them to line a walkway or to light a small pathway to a special event. The candlelight will glow through the cracks in the lanterns and reflect off the snow—they are beautiful on a snowy winter's night.

Materials:

- Butter knife.
- Tea light candle.

Directions:

1. Cut four rectangles from icy snow for each lantern you want to make.

2. Lean the four rectangles against each other in the shape of a square.

3. Place a tea light candle in the center of the lantern and light it.

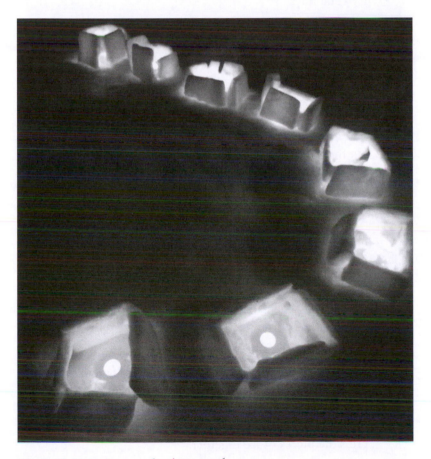

Figure 13.12 Ice Lanterns lit along a path

MINI CASTLES MADE WITH ICE CUBES AND ICICLES

This activity can be done any time of year, but the advantage of making these ice castles in winter is that kids who live in cold climates can keep them outdoors and add on to them throughout the winter. However, it's also a great activity to do with the kids on a hot summer day since they get the cooling benefits of playing with ice.

Materials:

- Recycled plastic containers (apple sauce, yogurt, pudding, and other snacks that come in small or divided plastic containers are perfect for this project).

- Other containers from around the house (medicine cups, funnels, milk cartons, etc.).

- Ice cube trays.

- Water.

- A freezer with plenty of room.

Directions:

1. Fill your containers ⅔ full of water.

2. Place the containers filled with water in the freezer. You can put them on a baking sheet if that makes it easier to transport and freeze them. You can also leave them outside to freeze if it's cold enough to do so. Allow the water to freeze overnight.

3. Take the containers out of the freezer. If you are doing this activity on a hot summer day, you only need to let containers sit out for a few minutes for the ice to start melting. If you are doing this activity in winter, or indoors, you may need to let the ice sit for 15 minutes or more for the ice to start melting. Either way, when the ice starts to melt you will be able to remove the ice from the containers. The ice will come out in the shape of the container it froze in.

4. Now you can build with the shapes. Bring out a bowl of ice cubes to go with the shaped ice. Press pieces of ice together till they stick. If they are not sticking well, then rub your finger over the spot where you want the ice to stick and then press the pieces of ice together.

5. If you need a sturdy surface to build on, you can use newspaper or a plate with paper towels on it. However, the ice might stick to the paper towels, so keep that in mind.

6. Kids can also use icicles from outside to add to their castles.

Chapter 14

BRING NATURE INDOORS

There are plenty of projects that kids can do indoors that incorporate nature-based materials and inspire nature-based play. Whenever you explore a natural space, make sure to bring back pine cones, rocks, sticks, driftwood, seed pods, and other natural found objects (as long as there are no rules prohibiting this) because you can use them later on in nature-based activities like the ones in this chapter.

Many of these supplies can also be purchased online but it's best to gather your own when possible.

CLAY INSECTS

Provide natural clay and nature-based materials for your child to create Clay Insects (and arachnids, etc.). Sticks can be bent to make legs, while leaves and flower petals can be used to make wings, and dried grass can be used as antennae.

Figure 14.1 Examples of Clay Insects

DRIFTWOOD CITIES

Collect various shapes of driftwood and allow them to dry. Use acrylic paint to create pictures of buildings, trees, and cars on the pieces of driftwood. When the paint is dry, assemble your city! Cities can be played with or used as decoration.

Figure 14.2 A city made out of driftwood

ABSTRACT STONES

Collect smooth stones and paint abstract images and patterns on them. Black and white acrylic paint works best if you want the stones to have an added 3D or illusion effect.

Figure 14.3 Abstract Stones and Stone Magnets

Materials:

- Smooth stones.

- Black and white acrylic paint.

- Paintbrushes.

- Varnish.

Directions:

1. Rinse the stones and allow them to dry.

2. Paint the top surface of the stones—use white paint for half of the stones and black paint for the other half (e.g. five painted white and five painted black).

3. Allow the paint to dry.

4. Use white paint over black, and black over white to make lines, polka dots, and other designs.

5. Allow the paint to dry.

6. Apply a thin layer of varnish over the painted areas and allow the varnish to dry.

7. Place in a bowl or on a shelf for display.

STONE MAGNETS

Small flat stones can be turned into magnets. These can be made for the home and for gifts.

Materials:

- Collection of small, flat stones.

- Acrylic paints.

- Paintbrush.

- Industrial-strength glue.

- Small, round magnets (not magnet strips).

Directions:

1. Rinse the stones and allow them to dry.

2. Paint pictures, words, or letters on the stones.

3. Allow the paint to dry.

4. Put a small dab of industrial-strength glue on the bottom of each stone (this step is to be done by adults only) and place a magnet on the glue.

5. Set the stones upside down to dry.

6. When the glue is completely dry, you can use the magnets.

INDOOR NATURE-INSPIRED GARLANDS

Garlands can be used to decorate a child's room or play space. They can be hung horizontally or vertically depending on what you are using them for. I especially love garlands for creating little nooks, like a fort. For example, garlands can be hung from a central part of the ceiling and then splayed outward to create a teepee shape. These enclosed spaces are wonderful spots in which to read to your child. You can also hang garlands to decorate for a special event, add to a theme for learning or reading at home, or to enhance imaginative play. If your child is passionate about space and stars, create star garlands to hang from their bedroom ceiling. If your child loves rainbows, make some raindrop garlands and a rainbow for their room. Other garland ideas are birds, snowflakes, leaves, flowers, lady bugs, or other insects.

PRISMS

If you have a window in your home that gets a lot of sunlight, hang a prism in that window. A prism will cast rainbows all around the room whenever sunlight hits it.

NATURE STATION

Find a space at home where the child can keep a collection of treasures they have found in nature. This can include items such as stones, shells, feathers, dead insects (e.g. a butterfly found on the side of the road), sticks, and other treasures they have come across. Your child will appreciate having a place to gather these treasures and show them to others. It will inspire your child to learn more about what they find and to appreciate the uniqueness of the items they collect. You can recycle small jars to keep the collection items in. Add a small magnifying glass, a nature journal, or nature guides to the station so your child can explore and learn even more about their collection of treasures.

INSECT HOUSES

Figure 14.4 A row of insect houses for a windowsill

If your child loves insects and tiny creatures, then they will love insect houses. Insect houses are tiny homes made from recycled cardboard which can temporarily house ladybugs, stink bugs, spiders, and houseflies your child finds in the home. The homes are not cages—

they are merely places for these insects to have a lie-down or a short stay. Create one home or make an entire neighborhood. Let your child know that insects can take care of themselves but it's a wonderful thing to provide a little home-away-from-home for them.

Materials:

- Paper.
- Scissors.
- Small cardboard boxes, such as recycled office supply boxes (e.g. for paper clips, staples, scotch tape), jewelry boxes, card boxes, and matchboxes.
- Glue.
- Crayons, markers, or colored pencils.
- Fabric scraps or tissues.

Directions:

1. Help your child with this step if necessary. Cut a strip of paper that will wrap around the box. This will cover up product details on the box and allow the child to decorate their house as they want. Also, cut out any doors or open spaces in the paper and box as needed.

2. Glue the strip of paper onto the box.

3. Cut a triangle from paper and glue that onto the top of the box, for the roof.

4. Allow the glue to dry.

5. Decorate the house.

6. Create cozy spots in the house for an insect. Use fabric scraps or tissue to make little "beds." Some kids love to decorate the inside of the house as well if the box allows for it.

7. Choose a spot, like a shelf or a windowsill, for your child to place the houses.

MINIATURE SANDBOXES

Outdoor sandboxes are a joy for many children, but you can make small sandboxes for indoor play as well.

Materials:

- Clean plastic container with a lid—you can choose the size, depending on your needs, but I prefer smaller ones that are approximately 12 in × 12 in (30 cm × 30 cm).

- Clean play sand.

- Small durable toys and figurines.

You can create themed sandboxes for play if you like. For example, if your child loves to play with construction toys, add stones and small construction trucks to the sandbox. If your child loves to pretend to cook, add measuring spoons, cups, spoons, and a bowl. Sandboxes can be brought out and used when needed. They can be stored for long periods of time.

WEB CAM WILDLIFE WATCHING

There are various live web cams on the internet for learning about wildlife. Viewers can observe animals in their natural habitats doing everything from feeding their babies to sleeping. If your child loves wildlife they may be interested in taking a moment each day to check in on a favorite animal. Puffins, penguins, bear cubs, and more can be observed at various websites.

Parent tips:

- Research the availability of wildlife web cams/live websites ahead of time. This way, you know exactly what your options are at the time and you can check the credibility of a site before getting your child invested in it.

- Some sites offer tips and suggestions for parents—read these when they are available. These pointers provide key suggestions that will help you discuss and learn about the animals you are watching.

- Check the website prior to each check in, without your child present. This way, if anything upsetting has happened to the animal since your last check-in, you will be better prepared to help your child deal with it.

NATURE SOUNDS

Purchase music or download an app that has nature sounds in it. Nature sounds include ocean waves, peeping frogs, rain, and so on, which can be soothing for some children to listen to at naptime or bedtime. Nature sounds can also be played during creative play time. If your child is pretending to be on a pirate adventure, for example, they could listen to ocean waves. If they are pretending to be a woodland fairy they could listen to sounds of the forest. In addition, nature sounds can accompany bedtime and read-aloud stories. If your child enjoys picture books, you can choose a theme based on nature and then play the same music or sounds in the background. For example, check out several books at your local library with a rain theme and then read these stories to your child while listening to rain sounds. Or read a stack of stories about frogs and turtles while listening to meadow noises.

CREATING WITH LEAVES

Leaves can be incorporated in several craft projects. Use leaves that are local to your area and that you are familiar with. I used oak and maple leaves for my projects because maple and oak trees are abundant where I live. But almost any tree leaf will work with these craft projects—just make sure you are using leaves that are non-toxic.

Leaf reliefs

Figure 14.5 Making Leaf Reliefs
Photo source: Verow

Making Leaf Reliefs is a standard craft activity for young children because it allows them to use crayons and colored pencils without needing to know how to draw. Kids can also help gather various leaves to experiment with.

Place a leaf between two pieces of paper. Then use a crayon or colored pencil to color over and across the area above the leaf. The details of the leaf will show up on the paper.

If you are a parent who enjoys crafts as well, save these reliefs for art projects of your own. They can be used in card-making, collage work, and altered art projects.

Painted leaves

Collect leaves that have a smooth surface and are non-toxic. Then use acrylic paints to paint on the leaves. Younger kids can paint with non-toxic acrylic paint colors and experiment with how it feels to paint on leaves. Older kids can choose to paint patterns, pictures, and even paint a letter on each leaf to spell out a word. Painted leaves can be made into a leaf garland as well—read the next section to find out how to make one.

Leaf garlands

Figure 14.6 A leaf garland

Leaf garlands can be used as decorations at special events and celebrations or to make a temporary teepee. The garlands only last a day or two because the leaves will dry up, so plan accordingly.

Materials:

- Non-toxic leaves.
- A hole punch.

- String.

- Acrylic paints and paintbrush (optional).

Directions:

1. Use your hole punch to make two holes at the bottom of the leaf—you will want to make one hole to the right of the stem and one hole to the left of the stem.

2. Repeat step 1 for each leaf you are using.

3. Cut a piece of string to the size you need for a garland.

4. Pull the string gently through the leaf holes—up one hole and through the second hole on the leaf. Then continue on with the next leaf and so on until you have a garland as long as you need.

5. Hang the garland. (I use tape to hang mine.)

If you want to make a leaf garland that spells out a word, then paint a letter on each leaf to spell out the word you want. Allow the paint to dry prior to making the garland.

Leaf teepees

Leaf Teepees are temporary structures that kids can make for indoor or outdoor play. Children gravitate to tiny fort-like spaces for imaginative play as well as quiet time. Leaf Teepees are especially enchanting because they smell like the forest and the trees they came from and they look quite magical. They are a nice break from making pillow and blanket forts.

Directions:

1. Make several leaf garlands that are about 6–8 ft (1.8–2.4 m) in length. The more garlands you make, the more covering the teepee will have, but ten is a good starting number for making a leaf teepee.

2. Gather one end of each garland string and tie them together in a knot.

3. If you are going to use the teepee outdoors, then find a tree branch that is sticking out horizontally. You can either tie the

garland knot around the tree branch or you can use a tack to secure the knot to the branch.

4. If using the teepee indoors, use a hook or tack to hang the knotted end of the garlands on a wall or ceiling.

5. Splay the garlands outward to create a teepee shape, leaving a space open for the entrance.

6. Secure the ends of the garlands. If indoors you can use tape, pillows, or a book to anchor the garland ends to the floor. If outdoors, you can use rocks or heavy sticks to anchor the ends.

Leaf pictures

Use a collection of leaves to create fun pictures. First you will need to gather a selection of various leaves—small, large, pointed, smooth, bumpy, feathery, and so on. Then draw pictures on paper using the leaves as part of the illustration. You can help your child with this activity by brainstorming what the different leaves look like, or what they remind the child of, prior to drawing.

Figure 14.7 Pictures created with leaves

CREATING WITH STICKS

Sticks can be used for so many different crafts and projects—collect them when you can and put them aside for later use.

Walking sticks

Figure 14.8 A walking stick created with nature-based materials

Walking sticks are sticks that are carried when you walk. The stick can be used to help with balance, to poke in puddles and grass, or just for the feel of something to hold. They can also be made into works of art. Walking sticks can be painted, carved, and decorated.

If your child wants to make a walking stick, you will need to go exploring to find one—look for sticks that are long, clean, and sturdy.

Next, provide materials for your child to decorate the walking stick. These materials can include clay, ribbon, string, yarn, paint, and nature-based materials such as feathers or shells. Allow your child to decorate the walking stick and then let it dry if necessary. Next time you go for a walk, your child can bring the walking stick along.

Painted sticks

Children can paint sticks of any size to use in imaginative play or in games. Sticks can be painted with patterns, designs, names, words, or painted to look like buildings and characters.

Pick-up sticks

Thin sticks can be painted different colors to be used as Pick-Up Sticks. Pick-Up Sticks is a game where a group of sticks is dropped to the ground and then players take turns removing the sticks from the pile. The object of the game is to see how many sticks can be removed in each turn without moving any of the other sticks. Player one tries to remove a stick from the pile. If they can move the stick from the pile without moving any other sticks, they take another turn. They continue their turn until they accidentally move another stick. Player two then takes a turn and does the same, and so on. The player who is able to remove the most sticks is the winner.

The sticks do not need to be painted in order to play the game, but can be painted to add color and design to the sticks. Painted sticks make the game a little easier to play with children because you can identify the sticks. For example, it is easier to say "try the blue-and-white, striped stick" rather than trying to describe a stick that looks like every other stick.

Stick wands

Sticks can be painted and decorated to look like magic wands, fairy wands, and wizard staffs. Cover a project area, such as a table, with newspaper. Then put out several clean sticks and craft materials you have on hand (e.g. glue, paper, ribbon, string, glitter, and paints). Have your child create their wand from the materials and use these wands in creative play.

Stick snakes

If you come across any curvy sticks, set them aside for making snakes. The snakes can be played with indoors or outside. Make sure the sticks you use are clean and free of insects. Then use acrylic paint to paint the sticks with designs and patterns. Paint a face at one end of the stick and allow the snake to dry.

Star sticks

Star sticks can be hung on the wall for decoration or glued to the tops of magic wands for added magic and detail.

Materials:

- Five sticks of similar length.
- Hot glue gun.

Directions:

1. Lay out the sticks in a star shape, starting with an "A" shape. The stick that crosses the "A" will extend outward.

2. Lay the other two sticks to make the final star shape—each stick will start at one bottom of the "A" and then reach diagonally toward the extended arms of the "A."

3. Move and adjust the star shape as needed and then use hot glue to secure each point of the star. Add hot glue as needed to hold the shape of the star.

4. If you are hanging a small- to medium-size star on the wall you can hang it from a pushpin. If you are using the star for a wand, secure it to the wand using hot glue.

Figure 14.9 Painted Sticks, a Star Stick, a Woven Branch, and a Yarn-Covered Stick

Woven branches

Branch weaving is a non-structured activity in which children experiment with various weaving styles and patterns. There is no right or wrong way to weave in this activity.

Materials:

- A small branch that has a "Y" shape to it.

- A variety of ribbons, string, and yarn with different colors and textures.

- Scissors.

Directions:

1. Tie a piece of ribbon, string, or yarn to one side of the stick where it branches off.

2. Weave the ribbon up and over, in and around the sides of the branches as desired. Remember, there is no right or wrong way to do this.

3. When your child wants to switch to a new color or material, tie the next piece on to the material she is using, and continue to weave.

4. Let your child continue to explore the motion and feel of this weaving, changing colors and textures as needed, until they say it is done.

5. You can tie the end of the final piece of ribbon onto the stick.

6. Woven branches can be hung as wall art or used in imaginative play. For example, woven branches can be used as a bed or hammock for a figurine, two racquet-shaped woven branches can be used to bat an acorn back and forth as a game, and a small Woven Branch could be used as a flying carpet for a small toy or figurine.

Yarn-covered sticks

If you knit or have leftover yarn in your home, this project will be a quick and inexpensive one for your child.

Directions:

1. Start by tying a piece of yarn onto the top or bottom of a stick. Then wrap the yarn around the stick to create a band of one color.

2. Tie on a new color of yarn and continue wrapping.

3. Repeat as necessary to create several bands of color.

4. When you have covered the stick, tie off the yarn by slipping it under a few rows and then making a knot.

Yarn-Covered Sticks can be used as pretend magic wands, maestro wands, mermaid flutes, and enchanted keys.

Log cabins

Build these miniature log cabins using water-based natural clay and sticks. Kids can use the cabins as a horse ranch, a house for a toy or figurine, or as a prop in imaginative play.

Materials:

- Newspaper.

- Water-based, self-drying clay.

- A variety of small sticks and twigs, acorns, and pebbles.

- Small milk or juice cartons (optional).

Directions:

1. Place the newspaper down where your child will be building—the clay can get a little messy.

2. Construct cabin walls by shaping the clay into equal-sized squares or rectangles, and then pressing twigs into the clay in rows.

3. You can also use the clay like "glue" to hold sticks together and create walls free-style.

4. Allow the walls to harden overnight.

5. Use clay to attach the walls of the cabin to each other. Lay sticks over the cabin or construct a pitched roof using clay and sticks.

6. Use sticks, acorns, and pebbles to add detail to the cabin.

7. Kids can also use the clay and sticks to make miniature animals and people.

8. Allow the clay to harden overnight.

CREATING WITH FLOWERS

Flowers can be an attractive medium for kids to create with because they offer many unique textures and colors. Pick flowers from a local park, your yard, or from the farmers' market, and try some of these flower crafts.

Pressed flowers

Pressed flowers are flowers that have been flattened and dried. They can be used in various craft activities.

Materials:

- Flowers.

- Sheets of paper.

- Thin tissue.

- Large book.

Directions:

1. Pick flowers you would like to press. The general rule is that the thinner and more delicate the flower, the easier it will be to press.

2. Take a sheet of paper and place a thin layer of tissue on top of it.

3. Lay a few flowers on the tissue, leaving space between the flowers.

4. Cover with tissue and another layer of paper.

5. Place in a large book.

6. Close the book.

7. Repeat until you have used all of your flowers.

8. Place a heavy or weighted object on the book. This will help to press your flowers.

9. Wait for a week.

10. Remove the flowers from the book. They should be flat and dried out by now. If not, put them back in the book for another few days.

Here are a few ideas for using pressed flowers:

- It helps to use tweezers to pick up the pressed flowers.

- Use decoupage glue to seal the pressed flowers onto a candle.

- Use decoupage glue to seal pressed flowers on bookmarks.

- Glue them onto handmade greeting cards or use in other paper crafts.

- Seal them onto plain glass ornament balls.

Flower pictures

Figure 14.10 Pictures created with pressed flowers

Your child can incorporate pressed and dried flowers in their drawings. The flowers can be glued into a picture to look like a person's clothing, accessories, or other item. See what ideas your child can come up with! All you need is drawing paper, crayons, pressed flowers, and glue. Your child can look over the pressed flowers and see if they "spark" an idea of something else that they look like. Then your child can draw around the flower and glue the flower into place when the drawing is done.

Hammered flower designs

Hammered Flower Designs create microbursts of natural color onto paper and fabric. Use the paper or fabric to make greeting cards, stationery, and bookmarks, or use them in collages and other art projects. This is a fun activity for kids who love to pick flowers, use a hammer, or make paper crafts.

Directions:

1. Gather some flowers, sturdy paper or white fabric, and a hammer. White flowers do not work well with this project so try to avoid choosing these.

2. Have your child place the flowers, one at a time, between several layers of paper or two layers of fabric.

3. Hammer over the flowers, which will transfer some of the flower's colors onto the paper or fabric.

4. Repeat as necessary to create splashes of color.

5. Allow the fabric or paper to dry afterward.

Bouquets in recycled containers

Go on an indoor scavenger hunt with your child to find recycled containers that could hold a small flower bouquet. Salt and pepper shakers, tin cans, spice jars, condiment jars, and coffee tins are examples of containers that can be used for bouquets.

Wash the containers and then pick the flowers. Trim the flowers and put them in your containers to make bouquets. Add water to the containers and then wipe the outside dry.

You can add decorative papers to the outside of the cans by cutting a strip of paper to wrap around the outside. The paper can be taped into place. You can even wrap a ribbon around the outside of the paper, if you like, and then tie it in a bow.

If you are using glass jars, you can use liquid leading and glass paint to add polka dots, stripes, or other patterns to the glass. Liquid leading does not contain lead. It is a thick, gray paint that you "draw" with that creates the outlines for your design. Once the liquid leading has dried, you can fill in the design with glass paints. Liquid leading and glass paint give a stained glass look to glass projects.

TINTED PUSSY WILLOWS

Figure 14.11 Pussy willows ready to be tinted with colored chalk dust

Pussy willows are the nickname of a shrub that comes from the willow tree family. In spring, the pussy willows start blooming with small, white, fuzzy blossoms that resemble bunny tails. You can tint these tiny blossoms using powdered chalk dust. I like to make rainbow-tinted pussy willows, starting with a red-tinted blossom at the top, followed by orange, yellow, green, blue, and purple.

Materials:

- Pussy willow stems (if pussy willows do not grow near you, you might be able to purchase them at a florist shop).

- Colored chalk.

- Newspaper.

- Small, dry paintbrush.

Directions:

1. Gently remove the hulls from the blossoms.

2. Rub a piece of colored chalk against the newspaper until you have a little mound of powder.

3. Roll the pussy willow blossoms in the chalk powder.

4. Gently brush the chalk powder into the blossoms, using the paintbrush.

5. Repeat with a different colored chalk for each stem.

CREATING WITH SEEDS AND LEGUMES

Mosaics and mandalas

Seeds and legumes can be used to "color" pictures and mandalas. Mandalas are designs created in circular form, used as an aid in meditation and relaxation. You can use mandalas for this activity or regular coloring pages, both of which can be printed from the internet or used directly from coloring books.

Materials:

- Coloring pages.

- Liquid glue.

- Tweezers.

- Various dried seeds, beans, and legumes (e.g. popcorn, kidney beans, pine cones, acorns, red lentils, and black beans).

If your child is younger, choose coloring pages that are basic and simple. Older kids might prefer a challenge, in which case use coloring pages with more detail.

Directions:

1. Choose an area near the center of the coloring page to begin.

2. Apply a thin layer of glue to the area.

3. Use tweezers or fingertips to add seeds or legumes, one at a time, to the area.

4. Continue filling the coloring page from the center outward, using different colored beans and seeds to fill the spaces.

5. When the picture is filled in, set it aside to dry.

Painted acorns

Acorns can be painted to create whimsical decorations. First, you will need to gather a collection of acorns for these projects.

Materials:

- Acorns—with and without caps.

- Acrylic paints.

- Small paintbrushes.

- Varnish.

- An oven and baking sheet.

Directions:

1. Collect acorns and acorn caps or order them online. Acorns are seeds from oak trees—the easiest place to find them is under oak trees in the fall.

2. If you collect the acorns yourself you will need to remove any that have holes in them. You will also need to bake the remainder of the acorns to remove mold and pests. See page 193 for baking instructions.

3. Try any of these painted acorn ideas:

- Paint all of the acorns the same color or shades of the same color. When they are dried, you can store them in a jar for decoration.

- Paint a small shape in the center of each acorn, such as a star or a heart. You could also paint the acorns red and then paint white hearts in the center for a Valentine's Day decoration.

- Paint patterns onto the acorns. Paint half of the acorns black and the other half white, then use the opposite color to make designs and patterns on them. Polka dots, checker squares, criss-cross lines, stripes, and swirls could be painted to create bold patterns for decoration.

- Paint faces onto the acorns.

- If you celebrate Halloween, you can paint the acorns orange and then paint Jack-o-Lantern faces onto the "pumpkins."

Figure 14.12 Acorns painted with faces and hearts

Pine cone forests

Miniature Pine Cone Forests are landscapes for creative play. Your child creates a small forest scene in a box (or pan) using the pine cones as trees. Clay is used to secure trees to the "ground" if needed, but some pine cones will stand on their own in soil or sand. If you have stones and sticks available, your child can also add those to the landscape or even build a small structure with them.

Once the forest and landscape have been created, your child can use it for various play. Toy recreation vehicles can race around, fairy tale figurines can explore, and figurine animals can create habitats.

Figure 14.13 A Pine Cone Forest with log cabin

Materials:

- Pine cones—the more variety the better.
- Clay.
- A cardboard box or pan.
- Soil or sand.

- Small sticks (optional).

- Pebbles (optional).

- Twigs (optional).

Directions:

1. Insert the bottoms of the pine cones (and any other objects to use as trees, such as twigs) in a ball of clay.

2. Press the "trees" to the bottom of the box or pan to secure them in place.

3. Place a layer of sand or soil along the pan or box.

4. Add pebbles or mounds of clay to create rocks and hills if you like.

5. Build and create any other structures you want to fit into your landscape.

6. See how many different ways you can use your forest for imaginative play!

REFERENCES

ASPCA (2013) *Domestic Violence and Animal Cruelty, How is Animal Abuse Connected to Domestic Violence?* ASPCA. Accessed on 8/1/2014 at www.aspca.org/fight-cruelty/report-animal-cruelty/domestic-violence-and-animal-cruelty.

LiveScience.com (Updated 2007) *Soil Bacteria Can Boost Immune System, Harmless Bug Works As Well As Antidepressant Drugs, Study Suggests.* Accessed on 2/4/2013 at www.nbcnews.com/id/18082129/ns/health-livescience/t/soil-bacteria-can-boost-immune-system.

Louv, R. (2008) *Last Child in the Woods, Saving Our Children from Nature-Deficit Disorder.* Chapel Hill: Algonquin Books.

Ober, C., Sinatra, S., and Zucker, M. (2010) *Earthing, The Most Important Health Discovery Ever?* Laguna Beach: Basic Health Publications, Inc.

Paddock, C. (2007) *Soil Bacteria Work In Similar Way To Antidepressants.* Medical News Today. Accessed on 2/4/2013 at www.medicalnewstoday.com/articles/66840.php.

Selhub, E. and Logan, A. (2012) *Your Brain on Nature: The Science of Nature's Influence on Your Health, Happiness, and Vitality.* Ontario: John Wiley & Sons.

ALPHABETICAL LIST OF ACITIVITIES

3D chalk drawings. 163

Abstract Stones 235

Acorn-cap finger puppets 191

Alphabet trees. .63

Animal totem shrines 55

Apple faces 190

Auroral displays 155

Backyard play kitchens 139

Beach bakery or bistro. 175

Beachcombing 177

Beach teepee 174

Bioluminescent mushroom hunting 156

Bird feeding 88

Bird treats 88

Boat building 207

Book-themed garden. 113

Bridge hunt 206

Bury yourself in the sand 178

Butterfly garden 112

Camping. 143

Cattail plants swords. 198

Chalk photo booth 164

Clay insects 234

Climbing trees 182

Collaged heart stones 76

Color bricks 165

Color-themed gardens 109

Community gardens 126

Construction sites and truck baths 202

Creating with flowers 252

Creating with leaves 241

Creating with seeds and legumes 256

Creating with sticks 246

Curio cabinet garden 105

Dam building 209

Dandelion puffs 64

Decorated tree formations 189

Domed plant worlds 128

Dragon tails and mermaid hair. 174

Dream catchers 52

Driftwood cities 235

Earth looms 81

Eat local and organic foods 14

Edge of the tide sculptures and drawings 170

Emotion/emoticon Stones. 28

Fairy and gnome gardens 118

Fairy house accessories and extras. 122

Fairy houses and gnome homes. 120

Fairy wings 193

Fantasy snow creatures 218

Farm visits 149

Firefly catching 156

Firefly talking 157

"Five senses" garden. 117

Flour lawn pictures. 195

Flower chains 197

Flower Crowns 197

Forest treasures 193

"Fossil" dig. 204

Four-leaf clover hunt 195

Frozen bubbles. 228

Frozen puddles. 229

Full moon walk 158

Garden rainbow. 112

Geocaching 143

Get your hands in the dirt 13

Giant gardens. 104

Go barefoot. 12

Go for a walk 13

Guided imagery 44

Hangman, hopscotch, and tic tac toe 174

Hopscotch and other blacktop games 167

Hum for a periwinkle. 175

Ice cube boats 202

Ice lanterns 230

Icy snow carving 230

Indoor nature-inspired garlands 237

Insect houses 238

Interactive chalk landscapes 161

Journey to the center of the Earth 101

Labyrinths and walking meditations 65

Leaf chains and garlands 187

Leaf crowns 185

Leaf Pile jumping 192

Letterboxing 141

Liquid sand sculptures .69

Lunar eclipses 155

Maple seed helicopters 183

Maple seed noses and beards 184

Medicinal Garden 106

Message Stones 74

Meteor showers 154

Mindfulness in natural spaces 71

Miniature outside worlds 136

Miniature sandboxes. 240

Miniature water world or marina. 201

Mini castles made with ice cubes and icicles 232

Mini lawn for your feet. 129

Mini sculpture gardens 126

Moon shadows 159

Moth feeding 158

Mud bricks. 205

Mud cakes and mud pies. 204

National and state parks. 145

Nature-based collections. 43

Nature-based urban art 166

Nature collages 54

Nature journals and sketchbooks. 133

Nature mobiles. 50

Nature sounds 241

Nature station 238

Nature-themed family portraits 33

Nesting shop. 89

Owl walk 157

Painting Stones with water 70

Pathways and patterns in the snow. 223

Pathways in fallen leaves 193

Pathways in the fields 196

Picnics 140

Pictures in the sand using found objects. 172

Pizza garden 107

Plein air art 135

Pooh sticks 208

Pop seaweed 176

Portable green gardens 63

Portable Zen garden. .61

Prisms 237

Public trails and historical places. 148

Puddle jumping 200

Puddle tracing with chalk 201

Rain Silhouettes 164

Random acts of kindness toward animals 90

River making 201

Rock art in your garden 125

Rock gardens 124

Salamander, snail, and bug hunt 209

Salsa garden 107

Sand angels 179

Sand castles 170

Sand sculptures 168

sand silhouettes 180

Scavenger hunts 133

Seed pod collecting 199

Shadow drawing. 97

Shadow puppets. 151

Shadow tag 173

Silly shadow portraits 173

Snow angels. 227

Snowball fight 227

Snowball sculptures 224

Snowflakes on a dark surface 228

Snowflakes on your tongue. 228

Snow forts and igloos 219

Snow furniture 223

Snow insects and animals. 215

Snow people. 213

Snow tunnels 223

Splash and wade 211

Square feet 79

Squirt clams 177

Stone magnets. 236

Stone stacking 68

Storytelling Stones. 21

Storytelling Stones in individual and group work 27

Storytelling Stones in sand tray work. 27

Striped Stone circles 177

Succulent-themed gardens 127

Talking sticks. 29

Teeny Tiny gardens 104

Terrariums 126

Tin can lanterns 152

Tinted pussy willows 255

Tree art 188

Tree meditation 99

Tumble and roll 194

Water painting 94

Web cam wildlife watching 240

Whimsical container gardens. 130

Willow branch crowns 189

Windowsill garden. 129

Wish books 39

Wishing wands. 30

Worry dolls and wish dolls. 36